AUG 1 8 '73

W9-BCP-257

3 0073 00039 5062

.335

Forman
Socialism

RETIRED FROM
NORTH KINGSTOWN
FREE LIBRARY
COLLECTION

27x
4/09

NORTH KINGSTOWN FREE LIBRARY
55 BROWN ST.
NORTH KINGSTOWN, R. I. 02852

SOCIALISM

STUDIES IN CONTEMPORARY POLITICS

Capitalism
Economic Individualism to Today's Welfare State

Communism
From Marx's *Manifesto* to 20th-century Reality

Socialism
Its Theoretical Roots and Present-day Development

By James D. Forman

Studies in Contemporary Politics offer wide-perspective examinations of major political and economic aspects of today's changing world. Using historical experience as a background, these books bring readers new understanding of the contemporary political scene.

STUDIES IN CONTEMPORARY POLITICS

SOCIALISM

Its Theoretical Roots and Present-day Development

James D. Forman

Franklin Watts, Inc.   New York ● 1972

Library of Congress Cataloging in Publication Data

Forman, James D
    Socialism; its theoretical roots and present-day
development.

    (Studies in contemporary politics)
    Bibliography: p.
    1. Socialism—History. I. Title.
HX36.F62   335'.009   72-6736
ISBN 0-531-02581-0

Copyright © 1972 by James D. Forman
Printed in the United States of America

For Lewis Gordon,
who has read most every book,
including mine, with enthusiasm.

Contents

SOCIALISM

Socialism Defined

Socialism has been called many things. It has been called an old religion, a modern ethic, a popular movement, a battle cry for revolutionaries, a drawing-room delusion of utopian philosophers, the salvation of the future, and the funeral pyre of civilization. In the United States, it has been a distasteful if not a dirty word. Sometimes it has been lumped with communism. Sometimes it has been seen as even more sinister, with a creeping capacity for engulfing our system of free enterprise.

Both communism and socialism are fundamentally economic philosophies that advocate public rather than private ownership, particularly of the means of production. Even here, distinctions begin. Karl Marx, on whose theories both philosophies are based, concentrated his attention on the industrial worker and on state domination of the means of industrial production. In practice, this Marxian dogma has largely been followed in Communist countries in conjunction with massive programs for the development of heavy industry, and the emphasis has been on production regardless of the wants or comforts of the individual. Socialism, occurring usually where industry has already developed, has concerned itself more with the welfare of the individual and the fair distribution of whatever wealth is available.

Communism has a rigid theology, and a bible, *Das Kapital,* that sees communism emerging as a result of almost cosmic laws. Modern socialism is much closer to the ground. It, too, sees change in human society and hopes for improvement, but there is no unchanging millennium at the end of the trail. Communism is sure that it will achieve the perfect state and, in this certainty, is willing to use any means, however ruthless. Socialism, confident only that the human condition is always changing, makes no easy approximation between ends and means and so cannot justify brutalities. This distinction in philosophy, of course, makes for an immense conflict in methods. Communism, believing that revolution is inevitable, works toward it by emphasizing class antagonisms. Socialism, while seeking change, insists on the use of democratic procedures within the existing social structure of the particular society. The upper-class capitalists are not to be overthrown but won over by logical persuasion. Such a process is far less dramatic, but in the long run world socialism has built on strong foundations. Its prospects are as bright as, if not brighter than, those of the ideologies with which it must compete in the twentieth century, for communism carries with it the fear of Soviet or Chinese domination, and capitalism the memory of colonial exploitation in vast and formative areas of the world.

In every idealized community that man has dreamed of throughout history, where human beings are pictured living in a harmony that transcends their natural instincts, there has been a touch of socialism. This tendency was particularly found in the Utopians of the early nineteenth century, whose basic motivation was the repudiation of the private-property system with its economic inefficiency and social injustice. Their criticisms rather than their projects would linger, for to a

SOCIALISM

man they offered a static solution in a changing world, and they completely misconceived the future of capitalism. Like Marx, they envisioned industrial capitalism becoming more oppressive and inhumane, and they could not imagine the mass of workers prospering in such a system. Yet the workers soon developed their own powerful organizations and began to bend the economic system to their own benefit. In parallel support of the labor movement were a variety of intellectual groups: the revolutionary Marxists, their revisionist fellows following Eduard Bernstein, the French Syndicalists, and, most practical and effective in promoting the political career of socialism, the English Fabians. This last group denounced revolution and accepted only political involvement within the given structure, hoping not to destroy the structure either secretly or by force, but to change it through persuasion and popular agreement.

Major strides were made toward this objective before World War I, a war that the Socialists, by philosophy pacifists, initially resisted, giving reluctant support only once the struggle had been joined. During the conflict public sentiment against pacifism tended generally to weaken the movement, but with peace, reaction set in. The cause of world socialism leapt forward, often overcompensating by adhering to revolutionary communism, which had taken fiery hold in Russia. The between-wars period saw the sudden spurt of socialism. Whether their leanings were democratic or totalitarian, all Socialists were bound together for a time in their resistance to fascism. The war that followed brought economic collapse close to victor and vanquished alike and, for the first time in many European countries, a majority support for socialism as the only path to well-organized reconstruction.

The decade following World War II was socialism's heyday. Economic planning and the nationalization of key industries were undertaken in many countries and to this day have not been repudiated, though a subsequent return to self-confidence in the private business community and among voters in general has frequently weakened the Socialist majority or reduced it to the status of opposition party. This political balance leaves most industrialized countries with a mixed socialist-capitalist economy. So long as there is no major world depression, this situation may remain relatively stable.

The consequences of World War II, particularly the coming of independence to many underdeveloped and formerly colonial nations, have opened vast territory for the rapid evolution of avowed socialism. African socialism, Arab socialism, and many other forms have been launched since the war. Most aspire to democracy, some profess it, but few have been willing or able to practice it except where the British political institutions have been well established.

Socialism, though concentrating on economic relationships, has always considered itself a complete approach to human society and thus a world rather than a national movement. In this respect as well, it owes much to Britain, for it was in London that the First Socialist International was organized in 1864 by Karl Marx. This radical leftist organization died after limping along for twelve years, by which time its headquarters were in New York. After the passage of about another dozen years, the Second International met in Paris to celebrate the anniversary of the fall of the Bastille. By this time, serious factions were developing: anarchists who wanted to burn everything, Communists who wanted to burn the establishment, and the democratic majority who favored lawful political action. Struggling for cohesion and peace right up until the First World War, socialism then lost its most powerful orator, Jean Jaurès of France, who was assassinated in Paris, where he was to speak out for world peace. Despite trench and barbed-wire barriers, a hard core of peace-hungry internationalists still managed to meet and exchange such slogans as "No annexations, no indemnities"; "Across frontiers, battlefields, devastated cities and countries—Workers, unite!"

Peace brought them all together again in Bern, Switzerland, but by this time the Soviet Union had been born. Russian Communists refused to attend the meeting on the grounds that the Second Socialist International opposed dictatorships and was an enemy to world revolution. Thus the Communist International evolved in opposition, while the Socialists went on to advocate the ''triumph of democracy, firmly rooted in the principles of liberty.''

The main objective of this Socialist International was permanent peace, an ironic and elusive goal in a time between two world wars. The Nazi attack on Poland in 1939 completely shattered the organization. In 1946, however, a Socialist Information and Liaison Office was set up to reestablish old contacts, and in 1951 the International was revived with a conference in Frankfurt, Germany, at which time it adopted a document, "Aims and Tasks of Democratic Socialism." A summary of these objectives gives a good picture of modern democratic socialism as it exists on paper in ideal form.

Always the first principle is nationalized ownership of the major means of production and distribution. Usually public ownership is deemed appropriate for the strategically important services, public utilities, banking, and resource industries such as coal, iron, lumber, and oil. Farming has never been considered well adapted to public administration and has usually been excluded from nationalization. From this takeover of the free-enterprise system Socialists expect a more perfect freedom to evolve, offering equal economic opportunity for all, the minimizing of class conflict, better products at less cost, and security from physical want.

At the international level, socialism seeks a world of free men living at peace. That freedom, at least from colonial overlordship, has largely been won. Peace throughout the world is a long way off, but, according to Socialist doctrine, putting an end to capitalism will do much to reduce the likelihood of war. Armies and business are seen to need one another, in a marriage of the weapons mentality and devotion to private profit through the economic exploitation of weaker countries. In this belief, American socialism coined the expression "Old soldiers seldom die, they fade into corporation jobs."

The United States remains the bastion of the free-enterprise system, which others may call, with less savor, capitalism. Socialism has long been regarded as a menace to the "American way of life." There is no question that Socialists argue for a change. Capitalism, in their opinion, makes for an unfair distribution of wealth, causing private affluence and public squalor. They also hold it responsible for environmental pollution and economic inflation. By curbing the absolute freedom of the private businessman or corporation, socialism hopes to satisfy all human necessities at the price of individual self-indulgence. Antitrust legislation, the graduated income tax, social security have all moved the United States toward the "Welfare State," which recognizes as its prime objective full employment and a minimum living standard for all, whether employed or not.

Even such taken-for-granted features of modern life as public schools and the federal postal service are relatively recent, socialistic innovations. Socialists applaud these programs, but, in what they regard as a sick society, these remedies seem to them only so much aspirin where surgery is needed.

While communism and socialism arose in reaction to the excesses of nineteenth-century capitalism, all three have matured in the past one hundred years. As a harsh father figure, capitalism has mellowed. While a sibling rivalry may continue to exist between communism and socialism, they have both become more tolerant of their parent. Officially, communism clings to the idea of revolution and the seizing of capitalist property by the state without compensation. Socialism accepts gradualism, feeling that a revolution, particularly in an industrial society, would be ruinous. In fact, Socialists and in some situations even Communists have come to realize that not all economic institutions function better in public hands. Private initiative and responsibility frequently offer benefits that redound to the public good. This is particularly true in the agricultural sector, where personal ownership and cultivation of land have always been deeply ingrained.

All socialism denies certain freedom. Couched in the most favorable terms, it deprives the minority of special economic privileges for the benefit of the majority. The more leftist, communistic socialism may deny the democratic process entirely. Traditionally defined, democracy holds to the idea that the people, exercising their majority opinion at the polls, will arrive at the common good by electing representative individuals to govern them. Communists would interpret this to mean the tyranny of an uneducated majority obliged to decide between a politically selected group of would-be leaders. There is no question that the democratic process has its limitations, but for want of a better method contemporary socialism accepts democracy as a major principle.

The expressed goals of modern socialism are commendable, but goals, of course, are easy to enunciate, particularly when there is no opportunity to carry them out in fact. The gulf between theory and practice is often insurmountable. The question remains whether, given the chance, socialism can bring about the perfect world it dreams of, or, short of this, a better world than now exists. Nowhere today does socialism exist in a pure and unchallenged form, but in many nations it has made impressive gains. What follows will be a survey of socialism, its theory, various forms, experiments, successes, failures, and its prospects in this rapidly evolving twentieth century.

British Socialism

All the great socioeconomic ideologies of the twentieth century are a direct product of the Industrial Revolution, the seeds of which were sown in Georgian England and brought to full capitalistic flower a century later. This process of industrialization was emulated with all due speed, ugliness, and oppression by western Europe and the United States. As the heartland of the industrial age, it is not surprising that Great Britain attracted many of the most influential social critics of the age. Hounded out of their own countries for their political ideas, it was in a tolerant, scholarly haven in England that Karl Marx and Friedrich Engels had time to write and publish the basic works of communism. And in Britain too, modern socialism has sprung from utopian roots into a system that today embraces most phases of British life and that provides an example of socialism for other nations to follow or avoid.

The Welfare State Until 1955 the term *welfare state*, indicating a government policy so organized that every member of the community is assured of his due maintenance, was not even in the dictionary. Not until 1941, when coined by William Temple, at that time archbishop of York, had the expression appeared in print, yet four years later it became official policy. Though Britain stood among the victors of World War II, her cities had been savagely bombed, her resources exhausted. She was tired of wars, and the old parties that seemed to encourage them. In June of 1945, with Germany down and Japan tottering, the British Labour party adopted the motto ''Let us face the future,'' and it achieved its first clear majority in the House of Commons. Labour's success came as a shock to Churchill's Conservative party, which expected some credit for winning the war. It was perhaps an even greater disappointment to Britain's small Communist party, whose doctrines of revolution defined away any possibility of success at the polls.

Leader of the Labour party and new prime minister was Clement Attlee, an Oxford graduate and lawyer of the Inner Temple. Having seen the poverty of London's East End as a student, he had been a convinced Socialist since 1907. His immediate socialist objectives were a planned economy, the nationalization of strategic businesses, including banking, and the granting of independence to as much as possible of Great Britain's colonial empire. Attlee was prime minister for six years and achieved most of his goals. In 1951 Churchill and his Conservatives received a narrow majority in the Commons, and for the next thirteen years the Labour party endured the secondary status of "Her Majesty's Loyal Opposition." Harold Wilson brought Labour back to power in 1964. Subsequently the Conservatives have returned, but despite keen opposition between the two parties the Conservatives have done virtually nothing to roll back the process of socialization that the Labour party set in motion just after World War II.

An obvious and easy first step then was the nationalization of finance. Owned by a body of private stockholders, the Bank of England was first chartered in 1694. It had always worked closely with the government. Like the Federal Reserve Bank in the United States, it served as custodian of the gold reserve and administrator for the national debt. On March 1, 1946, the government took over the Bank of England by a simple Act of Parliament. The former owners were compensated with government bonds, and a deputy and sixteen directors were appointed, primarily the same governing body that had directed the bank all along. The proceeding met little resistance since it put under national safekeeping an economy that was in trouble and made possible large-scale financial planning for the future.

Economic Planning Economic planning, such as the five-year plans associated with Soviet Russia and Red China, is at the heart of any Socialist government, and it is gradually being recognized as an unavoidable necessity in the complex economic world of today, regardless of the form of a country's government. In Britain, with a small land and a large population, planning was vital. It was no more than an extension of prewar guidance and the adaptation of wartime rationing into long-run peacetime goals. Characteristic of what had to be done were the guaranteed subsidies for various grain products. Cultivation of the latter had been so outstripped by the raising of livestock that one third of required fodder had to be imported. The government has made no effort to take over private ownership and operation of agriculture, but, through the guaranteeing of certain prices and wages, it has been able to guide the farming community as a whole along lines more beneficial to the national economy.

Economic planning has become a factor in urban development as well as in industrial growth. In 1932 a Town and Country Planning Act was passed that gave responsibility for decisions to the local government. A new act of 1947 gave control to the national government. An interesting sidelight was the creation of "new towns," with the treasury providing funds for the acquisition of sites and the building of roads, schools, shops, and homes. Several such complete towns have been built, mostly to relieve the congestion of the expanding London suburbs. Though the program in general has been a success, the Labour party, more moderate in deed than in dogma, has not pushed for the nationalization of title to all land but has acknowledged the deep psychological need of individual ownership.

Industrial planning has been put in the hands of a central economic planning staff. Production targets are set. Interested parties have been consulted, and in most cases cooperation has been achieved voluntarily, without the force or the threat of force that has been the mainstay of communistic "demand" economy. During the first six years of Labour party government many industries were nationalized, particularly those about which the following questions could be answered in the affirmative: Was the industry economically sick? Was it an industry vital to the nation? Could uniform rules of administration be applied?

Britain has been described as a lump of coal surrounded by fish, and the key to her industrial development in the nineteenth century and the prime source of her power in the twentieth was her wealth of coal. Coal was vital; yet after World War II the coal industry was shrinking, with lowering output, obsolete and failing equipment, and a deserting labor force. In July, 1946, the Labour government passed the Coal Industry Nationalization Act, and within a year the government became owner of one million acres and over eight hundred mining companies employing nearly a million miners, clerks, and managers. A National Coal Board was established to control the extraction and processing of coal. Under this board were nine divisional boards, and lower still were area general managers.

A tribunal established the value of the assets obtained and compensated the former owners with government stock. The government concentrated production on the better mines, and it modernized methods, so that a dying industry has been revived. Problems remain. While production has been stabilized, it has shown little growth. The miners themselves, despite improved working conditions and shorter hours, have not shown the sort of team spirit that the Socialist government has urged. Work is work, whether the owners are private or governmental, and the average worker sees his own well-being as distinct from the national interest.

In other areas, also, nationalization has taken place. The Electricity Act of 1947 transferred private and municipal power-generating stations to a Central Electrical Authority. The change has been successful, as has been the nationalization of the gas industry. In both cases, larger, more coordinated units have made for greater standardization and efficiency.

The nationalization of inland transportation, on the other hand, has met with mixed success. Early railroad lines, highways, and canals had mushroomed as the result of local custom, expediency, and private competition, making for a haphazard system and wasteful competition. In 1947 some sixty corporations in this field were nationalized, including the management that controlled seventy hotels, one hundred steamships, many dockyards, and three quarters of a million employees. As usual, the former owners were compensated with government stock. Unlike the other nationalization acts, this one was strongly opposed by the Conservatives. When they were restored to power, they undertook the interesting process of partial denationalization, particularly in the area of long-distance trucking. Some 37,000 trucks operated by the British Transport Commission had to be sold back to the public. The undertaking was made more difficult by the specter of a Labour party eventually taking them back. Though most were sold, terminal and garage facilities proved almost impossible to unload, and the government was obliged to maintain a competitive fleet under the British Road Service.

The greatest struggle developed over steel. The Iron and

Steel Act was passed in November, 1949, transferring securities of individual companies to the Iron and Steel Corporation of Great Britain. Otherwise, the individual corporate entities were left intact, retaining even the old corporate name and internal structure with a continuing board of directors. No changes were undertaken in the productive organization, and government intrusion concerned only long-term planning of capital expansion. Steel had never been in the desperate straits of the coal industry, and in the Conservative view, nationalization was only socialism for the sake of socialism, at a high cost in individual initiative and competitive spirit. However, such balancing of the practical against the theoretical remains basic to the development of democratic socialism and tends to characterize socialism's place between communism, which puts doctrine first, and capitalism, which is the outgrowth of practice.

Despite Labour's pledge to renationalize steel, the Conservatives set up a holding and realization agency to sell back steel stock to the public. Small companies negotiated directly with the former owners. Larger companies were sold through syndicates of investment bankers. Helped by a market rise and the Conservative election victory in 1955, stocks were disposed of without a loss of funds to the government. If nothing else, the procedure demonstrated that socialization could be a two-way process; that if need be, it could be undone. A returning Labour government, however, in 1964 committed itself to the renationalization of the bigger steel producers. It was by this time more realistic, though, and less anxious to absorb the private sector of industry simply for doctrine's sake.

Perhaps Labour's greatest and least-questioned triumph was the National Health Service, which became on the lips of American doctors and insurance agents the fighting phrase "Socialized Medicine." The objective of the British plan was a comprehensive program to diagnose and treat illness free of charge, or with a very minimal charge. Incorporated were the services of dentists, oculists, and surgeons. Those needing them could obtain hearing aids and even wigs when required by a pathological condition. The government took over some three thousand hospitals under the management of a minister of health. No doctor was forced to join the service, but 97 percent have done so. The few that remain outside cater to high-income patients who prefer the luxury of private physicians to the possible inconveniences of public service. Generally, the system has won favor even with the medical profession. Each doctor is given a number of patients. His fee is fixed for the first five hundred on the list, increased for the next one thousand as an incentive, and decreased thereafter to discourage overwork and possible negligence.

If the average doctor is guardedly in favor of the system, the patient and the public in general have few reservations. The consensus seems to be that, though the service isn't perfect, it is a better system than one in which the individual pays the bills. These bills are a real consideration at a time when hospital beds in the United States are in demand at $100 a day.

In a survey of the brief history of socialization in Britain, no final verdict can be reached at this time. Socialization has proved no panacea for the island nation that was once the greatest imperial power in the world. Income taxes are staggeringly high. The Labour party has lost its magic aura. Some of its programs have worked, others haven't. Perhaps these measures were all that brought Britain out of the wreckage of war; perhaps not. Unfortunately, national government is not an area susceptible to controlled experimentation. The results of untried alternative procedures can only be guessed at, but, good or bad, practical democratic socialism has come to Great Britain and it is working.

The Origin of Socialism Socialism as applied in post-war Britain was no instant creation. It had had political leaders, such as Ramsay MacDonald in the 1920s, and earlier theorists.

The ideal ethic of justice and charity that motivated socialism went back as far as the Old Testament prophets Hosea and Isaiah, emphatically strengthened by Jesus' teaching of an ideal based on love. In England, this moral flame was rekindled by John Wycliffe in the fourteenth century. Perfect communism was what God had ordained, but government was an expedient made necessary by the fall of man. Wycliffe's disciple, John Ball, typical of so many who have tried to breathe life into pacific ideas, translated them into violent action. He became a leader of the Peasants' Revolt against King Richard II. It came at a time when living conditions were unbearable, taxes were high, and the nobles were encroaching upon the peasants' common pasture. This first practical striving for common ownership failed, and Ball died on the gallows.

Sir Thomas More's Utopia Thereafter for quite a while, a socialist paradise was left to the philosophers. Having heard stories of native islanders who had no use for pearls or gold, Sir Thomas More, in the sixteenth century, invented a sailor by the name of Raphael Hythloday. He set him ashore on the island of "Utopia," meaning "Nowhere." The resulting work of that name was an indictment of warring kings, of harsh punishment, and of the institution of private property. More's *Utopia* featured an agricultural economy where all goods were gladly deposited in a central warehouse from which each man could withdraw sufficient material for his needs. To bring gold into disrepute, that metal was made to fashion slave chains. The slaves were the criminal element, who did the undesirable work in a paradise where each honest citizen had a vote.

Other ideal communities would later be envisioned, but the word *utopia* would remain in use to this day. Francis Bacon put forward his New Atlantis, which focused scientifically on a so-called Solomon's House, a college full of technicians and inventors who turned out new discoveries as they were needed. Though property was individually owned under Bacon's system, all knowledge was shared. These early utopians may be quickly dismissed, since their schemes were beyond practical application. Karl Marx was one of the most sarcastic in his disavowal of this dreamy past, but there is much of the utopian in his own vision, particularly the classless society of the future, the millennium, which would bring final bliss and harmony to the world. But Marx's ideal state, unlike the others, has been as Wycliffe was to Ball, a catalyst to more realistic thought and often to bloody action.

Throughout the Middle Ages, the poor were considered to be poor by God's will. The condition therefore bore no disgrace and gave those more favorably blessed the chance to practice charity. The destitute lived in hovels, roamed the woods, and were not a very great problem until the sixteenth century brought rapid population growth. In 1601, the first Poor Law was enacted. It undertook to remedy the condition of the poor, for by this time divine sanction had vanished. Poorhouses were established to care for the aged, the sick, and the insane, while work programs were set up for the able-bodied. Good or bad, this Elizabethan law endured for over two hundred years, well into the Industrial Revolution.

Even during the Cromwellian Civil War, the institution of private property remained solidly entrenched despite the efforts of one Gerrard Winstanley, who urged a communistic return to nature. He and his followers, to illustrate this process, concentrated on plowing up commons and parks. By totally digging up and manuring a particularly large hill in Surrey, they returned it to its condition at the time of creation. Considering them harmless, Cromwell let them turn the soil until the movement died of exhaustion. They are remembered now only in bibliographies as "the Diggers." Another more practical group of the Cromwellian era, and one often regarded as a prototype of later British and European socialist evolution, was known as "the Levellers." Of all the institutions that stood in the way of human equality the monarchy seemed to them the highest and most in need of leveling. To this end their agitation was in part responsible for the execution of King Charles I.

With the advent of the Industrial Revolution, digging was hardly enough. The cities of Britain were being turned into sinkholes, and, recalling the plagues of old, the powerful and well-to-do set about improving sanitary conditions. This led to the 1834 Poor Law amendments and to various public health legislation aimed at disposing of sewage, paving streets, and pulling down the worst slums. The administration of public health was placed in the haphazard hands of hundreds of local agencies and volunteers, but it was a start.

A Scottish schoolmaster, Thomas Spence, dreamed of land held in common by parishes that would rent it out to farmers. From this rental the government would derive a single tax. So sure was Spence that this would make for a complete solution that for years he peddled his tracts on street corners, but to no avail. Less subtly, William Godwin wanted to abolish government, and private property along with it. Just how to do it, he left rather murky. The poet Shelley protested without offering any solution:

The seed ye sow, another reaps;
The wealth ye find, another keeps;
The robes ye weave, another wears;
The arms ye forge, another bears.

Robert Owen Robert Owen, also, had a solution, and though Friedrich Engels would describe him as a utopian reformer of "almost sublime and childlike simplicity," one application of his technique actually worked. Born the son of an ironworker in North Wales in 1771, Owen had become the superintendent of a Manchester cotton mill before he was twenty. Later, he bought his own cotton mill in Lanark, Scotland, a town ridden with poverty, crime, drunkenness, child labor, and one-room family dwellings. Into this deprived setting Owen brought immense energy, a good heart, and a theory that was novel at the time. He believed a human being to be less a product of his own constitution than of the conditions that surround him. To change a man, one need only change his environment. With this conviction, Owen began the town's transformation to New Lanark. He enforced strict rules of sanitation, supplied the workers' necessities at cost, built decent houses, curbed drinking, and prepared kindergartens for the children of workers. During the depression of 1806, when mills throughout Britain were closed down, he went on paying his employees' wages in full. The result was indeed a transformation, and New Lanark became world-famous for its cleanliness, temperance, and business success. Students of social problems came to study it from all over Europe.

This was Owen's great triumph, but he had further plans. Breathing the heady air of success, he was prepared to tackle the world. The results were sadly Quixotic. He broke his lance repeatedly on the windmill of parliamentary inaction. Hopefully, he campaigned for the twelve-hour day and to have prohibited the employment of children under ten. He conceived a scheme for communal living, with meals and recreation to be taken in one large building surrounded by farmland. There would be separate farm and factory buildings. These independent economic units, consisting of from five hundred to two thousand people, would supersede the existing state. Not even British workmen liked his idea, though, and Owen had to go as far away as Harmony, Indiana, to set up an experimental community. It failed. Undaunted, he kept up the fight. He planned trade unions and cooperatives but failed repeatedly in his projects, apart from New Lanark, though in years to follow, through other means, the abuses that disturbed him would be eliminated. It is not without reason that Robert Owen has been christened the father of British socialism.

The Cooperative Movement Reform arrived in many packages, some religious, some philosophical, others purely practical. Most influential among the latter was the Consumers' Cooperative movement, which was a socialistic experiment in joint ownership. It began modestly with an organization of Fenwick Weavers near Glasgow in 1769. This approach to counteracting the capitalist monopolies received new impetus in 1843, when twenty-eight weavers and other workers met in the Chartist reading room in Rochdale, near Manchester, and decided to set up a retail store owned and managed by members and run without profit. After a year of saving, these men rented the ground floor of an old warehouse on Toad Lane and stocked their store with $70 worth of flour, oatmeal, butter, and sugar. The principles of operation were simple. Each member had one vote in cooperative affairs. Capital would be invested at a fixed rate, and surplus would go to members as dividends after paying for commodities and upkeep. By 1895, membership had reached twelve thousand, and other stores were started. From selling the simple necessities of life, cooperatives branched out into the purchase of land so that raw materials might be produced. With the need for credit, banking was undertaken, then insurance and industry. Today, with membership open to all, over twelve million Britons are members of cooperatives.

The movement has by no means been localized. The cooperative system has been encouraged in socialistic Sweden and involves almost half of the population. Most of Israel's agriculture and some industry, housing, and passenger transportation services are under such a system. The movement has spread to the Western Hemisphere, where it is particularly strong in Argentina, Chile, Mexico, and Canada. The United States, since the end of its pioneering era, has seen a steady growth of cooperatives, particularly in the form of credit unions and farm marketing. World membership in such groups is estimated now at over 200 million, an expansion beyond the wildest imaginings of a few impoverished weavers who pooled their assets in order to compete with the capitalistic giants of their day.

The cooperative movement has attracted certain latter-day theorists who would like to expand the idea into a complete socialized way of life, with cooperative ownership of all wealth, governments, and presumably armies. The most idealistic among them would credit the cooperative spirit with the will and the way to eliminate all competition, and wars as well. Such views are utopian and far from realization, but in terms of economy and financial benefits to the small consumer, the cooperatives should not be underrated. They operate without profit, and costs have also been reduced by eliminating the middleman, often even the manufacturer. The quality of goods sold has generally been improved, along with the working conditions of those employed.

Unlike communism, which has always professed materialistic atheism, a leading segment of democratic socialism has had from the beginning a religious theme. In Britain, Christian socialism was begun by two clergymen, Frederick Maurice and Charles Kingsley. These men despised laissez-faire industrialism and saw the human race as one great family. They launched their campaign in 1848, the year before Marx settled in London. It was generally a period of revolution and unrest. Ten years before, a Workingmen's Association had drawn up a "People's Charter" that guaranteed reforms along socialist lines. Growing agitation followed, and, one day in 1848, Chartist workers began milling about in London, which had been placed under military rule. Carrying a placard bearing a message signed "a working person," the pair of clergymen arrived in time to address and pacify the crowd. Subsequently they published a paper entitled *Politics of the People*, but their money soon ran out.

Later Kingsley was to write *Cheap Clothes and Nasty*, a book that pictured Mammon, the cruel capitalist, adorning his body with the flesh of men and women. Kingsley's book was an indictment of capitalism in general and of the so-called sweated industries in particular. "Sweating" was a system whereby laborers were obtained for clothing manufacturers. The "sweater" not only obtained the workers, he also provided them with housing, but charged so much that they fell into hopeless debt. Crowded together, sometimes ten to one dark and tiny room, the workers were obliged to work where they ate and slept and often died.

Some reforms followed, but along with them came a reaction on the part of the upper classes. The clergymen were accused of a morbid desire for notoriety, and about 1853 the Christian socialist movement went into gradual decline. It revived in the 1880s and gained a foothold in the growing Labour party to such an extent that George Lansbury, Labour party leader in the 1930s, would write, "Socialism, which means love, cooperation and brotherhood in every department of human affairs, is the only outward expression of a Christian's faith."

While communism has tended to flow in a single channel, thereby gaining strength at the sacrifice of flexibility, democratic socialism has cut many lesser and divergent courses. By no means the least important, particularly to socialism's development in Great Britain, is the intellectual approach. There was no keener mind at work on social problems than that of John Stuart Mill. As an economist, Mill speculated upon the idea that wealth increased of itself without effort on the owner's part, and upon the feasibility of state appropriation of wealth for the good of society. His convictions grew gradually more socialistic until, at the time of his death, he was midway through writing a book on the subject.

The Fabian Society Mill had been dead ten years, Karl Marx only a few months, when an American, Thomas Davidson, addressed a group of young British scholars. By Davidson's time, the workers' revolt against capitalism expected by many Communists and Socialists showed little sign of materializing. Capitalism was bigger than ever, and so were the young trade unions. Davidson urged his youthful and enthusiastic listeners to involve themselves in the contest for the good of all society. The response was keen. In early 1884, the Fabian Society was founded.

Named for the Roman general Quintus Fabius Maximus, known as Cunctator, "The Delayer," the Fabian Society was to become one of the leading forces in British socialism. With such distinguished members as George Bernard Shaw and H. G. Wells, it adopted the following motto: "For the right moment you must wait, as Fabius did . . . but when the time comes, you must strike hard, . . . or your waiting will have been vain and fruitless." Though they went on to great accomplishments, they never lived up to this slogan, for it was not in their nature to strike hard. It was theirs to persuade the upper and middle classes of the practical advantages of socialism. The Fabians did not raise provocative placards—''Down with capitalism, up with the Proletariat''—they simply reasoned for cooperation as a substitute for competition in the conviction that the economic side of complete democracy was socialism.

Early capitalists had supervised their own businesses on an immediate basis. With economic development, managers replaced owners. Great corporations were formed, stock was sold publicly, and those at the top were as much employees as those at the bottom. The true capitalist had thus eliminated himself from the system. The Fabians, believing in the evolutionary nature of socialism, argued that the next step was for control to be in the public interest. Though public control was their objective, they did not look for its fulfillment through force and revolution. Instead, they met with key men in business as well as in government. They soberly lectured to the working class. Wisely, the Fabians did not make enemies of the establishment. They published such modest tracts as ''Municipal Milk and Public Health," and "Life in the Laundry," which reduced questions of principle to matters of fact. The times were ripe for their modest message and they moved in step with the evolving society, achieving reform without resentment.

During the 1920s the Fabian Society experienced considerable internal dissension, and many of the younger members left to join the Guild Socialist movement. The war brought a resurgence of support that reached a peak in 1943, when there were 3,600 members under the chairmanship of G. D. H. Cole. At this time, Cole described the society's purpose as being that of formulating and giving publicity to new ideas whether or not they conflicted with Socialist orthodoxies. Socialism, as he saw it, was simply a set of guiding principles that needed reassessment in the light of continually changing social conditions and needs. There could be no greater danger to its viability than the formation of irrefutable dogmas. Today the Fabian Society continues to exist with its purpose unaltered. Though its membership has never exceeded a few thousand, its importance can be measured by the fact that of the 394 Labour party members elected to Parliament in 1945, 229 were society members.

The British Labour Party   The vehicle in which Socialist ideas eventually rode to political expression was, of course, the British Labour party. This party was the natural outgrowth of the trade-union movement, which developed among workers in their efforts to achieve a bargaining position with their employers. Membership outside the trade unions was furnished by Socialists, the Fabians, and those who believed as they did. It was in the 1890s that the first efforts were undertaken to form the Independent Labour party. The objective was collective ownership and control of the means of production. Until the Socialist element had its persuasive say, the workers had no use for social reform or parliamentary action. They simply wanted to shoulder their way to economic power, but the Socialist group had convincing talkers.

By 1900, agreement had been reached between Socialists and trade unionists, and a "Labour Representative Committee" was set up. Six years later the British Labour party put forward its first candidates for Parliament, and twenty-nine were elected. Within a decade the Conservatives were swept out and the Liberals moved in, with Lloyd George as Prime Minister. Lloyd George brought with him an Old Age Pension Act, and, after studying the German social insurance scheme established by Bismarck, he set up a National Insurance Bill in 1911 that provided compulsory contributory insurance against loss of health and unemployment. This was the heyday of the Liberal party, which diminished thereafter, not so much through failure as through success in achieving its principles. It simply had nowhere to go. The Labour party, however, was brand new, and it had worlds to conquer. Before World War I, it forced through Parliament a Trades Disputes Act, which allowed picketing and was virtually a Magna Carta for the British workingman.

Socialists, rather like their Communist cousins, have tended to regard war as an affair of kings and capitalists. World War I was seen in this light, and consequently the Labour party was weakened by a pacifism-versus-nationalism split in its membership. The rift lasted only as long as the war. Its end was seen as a victory for brotherhood and future peace and as the defeat of authoritarianism, feelings that combined to strengthen Labour's position. In 1918, the party adopted a program called "Labour and the New Social Order," which boiled down to fraternity, not fighting, and cooperation, not competition. In practical terms this meant a minimum wage, unemployment insurance, and certain guarantees of education, leisure, and health. Having largely absorbed the Liberal party, Labour, for the first time, formed a cabinet in 1924 under the prime ministership of Ramsay MacDonald. It lasted only nine months. Again, in 1929, Labour received the most votes, though not a clear majority. Once more their dominance was uncertain and brief, with MacDonald defecting in 1931 to a Conservative and Liberal coalition.

The 1930s were an unhappy time for the British Labour party. It was out of power in a world gone mad. It urged the government to aid Loyalist Spain against the Fascists, and the government put an embargo on arms. It warned the government to beware of Hitler. When the war came, Prime Minister Chamberlain soon resigned in despair. Churchill formed a war coalition government that included Labour under the leadership of Clement Attlee. This time, there was none of the reluctance that had accompanied World War I. The issue was clear. Britain was fighting for her life against power-mad fascism. A few years later came victory over the Axis powers and Labour rode the tide, receiving 393 out of 640 seats in the House of Commons, its first clear majority. Since then, the Labour party has been a force in government, whether in power or in opposition. It remains the repository for socialist thought and strength: not the complete and radical socialism of the Utopians, or of Robert Owen, or even of the Fabians, but realistic, pragmatic socialism, in fact, and a basis for study and immitation throughout the world.

A curious imitation takes place in Ireland, which has never aspired to things English. Nor has Ireland the natural elements for socialism. The middle class is small. There is very little industry, so little that lack of factory smoke has been featured in tourist posters. Only since the mid-1950s has industry shown signs of life. Socialism is an English and unpopular word, yet the government operates its own radio and television stations, not to mention the only electric power and utility company, the railroads, and the sugar-beet industry. A third of all private industry is subsidized by the government. Help is given the home builder and the person in need of medical assistance. Education is free. Though a comprehensive health plan is lacking, the government does offer a health insurance plan. Call it whatever they want, the very independent Irish, while snubbing "Mother England," have adopted many of the elements of English socialism.

Continental Europe

Principal powers and traditional rivals in Europe are France and Germany. Both experienced in succession the Industrial Revolution, capitalism, and reaction on the part of the working classes and their intellectual leaders; and both countries have experimented with socialistic measures in the twentieth century. Here the similarity ends. France had already experienced her social revolution in the eighteenth century before the flowering of capitalism, a flowering that was never as complete there as in Germany. With the unrest that preceded the French Revolution had come the first of France's Utopians. Along with other political philosophers, they contributed to the social ferment leading up to the bloody rebellion against the callous opulence of king and courtier.

Early French Utopians   Utopian dreams thrive on disillusionment such as that of François Emile Babeuf. Known as Gracchus Babeuf (after the Roman brothers and tribunes who tried to institute reforms), he was an idealist crushed by the world's cruelty. During the French revolution he published his communistic paper, *The Tribune of the People*. In it Babeuf suggested nationalizing the property of businessmen and depriving individuals of inheritance rights. All would eat and dress alike. Children would be taken from their parents and communally raised, a cheerless answer to cheerless times. Accused of plotting against the revolutionary government, in 1797 he went to the guillotine. When the blood of the revolution had been washed away, the peasants and the urban working people still bore heavy burdens under the stern empire of Napoleon.

The next French utopian, Comte Henri de Saint-Simon, was an optimist. Each morning, under instruction, his valet aroused him with the exhortation ''Arise, Monsieur le Comte, you have great deeds to perform.'' This reminder was not wasted. Saint-Simon took an active part in the American Revolution at the siege of Yorktown. He also became president of a Paris commune during the French Revolution, an episode that left him impoverished but undaunted. Saint-Simon insisted that the world needed a guiding principle, and that it must come from an industrial-scientific system. Under the spiritual direction of men of science, industry would fall to public ownership, and each man would labor according to his ability and be rewarded according to services rendered. The entire structure was to follow military lines and was nearly as extreme and drastic as Babeuf's schemes.

Saint-Simon's contemporary in the early nineteenth century, Charles Fourier, had the notion that work could be fun if rightly organized, and that, where truly dirty work was concerned, children could be induced to perform it through a happy spirit of emulation and service. It had to be done voluntarily in any case, without state pressure. Strangely enough, Fourier attracted a wide following. His mission began during a time of famine in France when he was commissioned to dump a great cargo of spoiled rice from a ship into the sea. The owner, relying on hunger to drive up the price, had kept it too long.

Fourier's ambition was to start an experimental community, called a phalanstery, of some four hundred to two thousand people living in a central apartment house surrounded by farmland. Reward for labor would depend on the importance of the labor done. For instance, garbage collecting, an essential work, would be highly paid. Utterly convinced that his experiment would succeed and thereby convince and change the world, Fourier advertised in the papers for a wealthy philanthropist to sponsor the program. He offered to interview said philanthropist at twelve noon precisely at his home, and for twelve years at the designated hour he awaited this messiah's coming. None came. Some voluntary converts tried out phalanstery living and failed. After his death, many disciples organized such colonies. The most famous for its intellectual membership was the American one at Brook Farm in Massachusetts, but, like the others, it had only brief success. Indirectly, however, Fourier's writings did have permanent influence, particularly in bringing about factory and sanitary reforms.

Two other utopians deserve mention, Louis Blanc (1811–1882), and Pierre-Joseph Proudhon (1809–1865). Blanc was the first utopian Socialist to try to implement his ideas through the existing political machinery. He was the first to shift his appeal from the prosperous to the suffering worker. Instead of competition, man should learn brotherly cooperation, and his first suggestion to this end was the establishment of social workshops that would offer guaranteed work for all. Blanc's influence was such that a governmental experiment was made with his shops, but this attempt failed under the administration of bitter enemies who fatally sabotaged performance. While Blanc had tried to work within the government,

Proudhon bitterly contended that all forms of government were bad. His final objective was anarchy, the absence of master, servant, and private property.

France's most valuable contribution to socialist thinking occurred within the growing trade unions. The French Revolution had achieved very little liberty for the worker, and anti-combination laws slowed the development of trade unions. Not until the 1860s did a large-scale movement get under way. Again progress was slowed by involvement in the Franco-Prussian War. After France's humiliating defeat, a new provisional government was formed. French workers, fearing the monarchical tendencies of the National Assembly, established the so-called Paris Commune of 1871. Its objective was a federation of such communes, but its life was short and bloody and ended in massacre when government forces stormed the city.

Syndicalism Thereafter, militant trade unionism took three distinct paths. One, led by Jules Guesde, had drifted toward the teachings of Karl Marx. Another favored anarchism in the belief that all government was bad and its destruction the only recourse. A third development, the most important one, put faith in progress, not through politics, carried if need be to insurrection, but through devastating economic pressure. The Confédération Générale du Travail foresaw French laboring men banded together in vast trade unions, called syndicates, which, through direct action, would eventually gain control of the means and processes of production. Direct action was favored over political and intellectual discussion. The appeal was directly in the workingman's instincts and not, as with Marxian theory, to a philosopher's concept of what those instincts should be. Eventually, the syndicate was to be the core of all social organization and the prime unit of influence in society. Through the syndicate the worker could enter into a struggle with his employer by way of boycotts, minor sabotage, and, always glowing at the end of the Syndicalist rainbow, the general strike. From the first, Syndicalists dreamed of a vast, paralyzing general strike, a peaceful but relentless folding of arms that would starve out the capitalists. Government would be replaced by a Bourse du Travail, a city trade union council.

Very little practical thought was given to the state of workers' stomachs while the capitalists were starving. There was no real need to do so, for the general strike was an emotional, never a practical undertaking, although the workers thought it to be. Georges Sorel, one of the leading theorists of syndicalism, admitted as much when he said that, in fact, no general strike was likely to take place. Rather, it was a rallying cry, or at most a distant promise, like the promise of Christ's second coming or of the Communist millennium. It had done its job as long as the idea preserved faith in the future and fear in the hearts of capitalists.

Despite the indefinite postponement of the general strike, syndicalism had a surprisingly long life. It was never stronger than shortly before World War I, when a large-scale railroad strike threatened to spread. Martial law broke the strike and the rank and file suffered their first real disillusionment. The war absorbed syndicalism, and by the time peace came again, there was an infusion of Socialist membership, which had never favored the general strike. Syndicalism drifted slowly into the more orthodox political arena, campaigning for a forty-hour week and a minimum wage.

Labor syndicalism, owing to its earlier antipolitical stance, never achieved real union with the French Socialist party, nor did French socialism itself present a united front, as did the British. Nevertheless, at the onset of World War I, the French Socialist party had a respectable membership in the House of Deputies under the leadership of Jean Jaurès. The war changed everything. Jaurès was assassinated, and many members defected to form a Communist party. In 1923, Léon Blum, the son of a successful silk ribbon merchant, took over leadership of the remaining Socialists, who had been steadily moving toward the Left. Representation grew, and, with the mounting Fascist threat in the 1930s, the Socialists joined the Communists in a popular front. Together they held sufficient seats for Blum in 1939 to head a coalition cabinet. It put through several measures favorable to the trade unions: collective bargaining, provisions for a wage increase, nondiscrimination against trade unionists. The coalition survived only until 1938, when Daladier's "Government of National Defense" was formed.

The Second World War destroyed any accord between the Socialist and Communist parties in France, and peace did not restore it. Neither party was helped by the war. The pact between Russia and Germany in 1939 had shaken the Communists. The suppression of the Hungarian Revolution in 1956 rattled the party's aging bones once again, and though today the Communist party in France may point to a large membership, it is not a party of revolution. Rather, it is one of interest in material well-being, a nonrevolutionary group that has joined the "haves," wanting more but not at the risk of losing all.

The Socialist party, though sacrificing a part of its membership to a splinter group calling itself the Unified Socialists, did profit from some of the same postwar hope that swept British socialism to power. France was desolated in 1945. People were reduced to wearing wooden shoes, and the old complacent reliance on the economic self-sufficiency of the rural peasant town was shattered. People spoke of heavy industry, of "Americanizing" the economy with American funds but "with a difference." The aircraft and munitions industries had already been nationalized in the 1930s, not because of socialist theory so much as for expediency to meet the Nazi threat. In 1946 Felix Gouin, a Socialist leader, became president. He proceeded to nationalize mining, power facilities, insurance, and the Bank of France, all practical measures to put the nation back on its feet. Another Radical-Socialist-led coalition, headed by Pierre Mendès-France, ruled briefly in 1956 and 1957.

Then Charles de Gaulle took over. De Gaulle and his disciple and successor, Georges Pompidou, have not undone the process instigated by the Socialists. They have used it to build up French industry and prosperity within a planned economy under the supervision of an economic planning commission. Internationally, though brandishing a nuclear stick in a manner counter to Socialist pacifism, de Gaulle went along with Socialist policy in liberating, sometimes reluctantly, most of France's colonial possessions.

Socialism in Germany In Germany, the clamor for social justice began late. Early voices of protest were repressed. Radicals like Karl Marx were run out of the country, and the first workingmen's associations made little impression until the revolutionary days of 1848. A wide range of reforms was then being demanded by the lower classes throughout Europe, and when a Paris demonstration was fired upon late in February, trouble spread. About three weeks later, Metternich was forced to flee Austria when students urged the people on to denounce his cruel despotism. Other countries experienced similar upheavals, and spontaneous uprisings occurred throughout Germany. In Berlin, the populace demanded that the king grant Prussia a constitution, and a national assembly was called for that purpose. However, passions all too quickly expended themselves. In Paris, the army put down the republican workers savagely, and four thousand of those who had been shouting "Bread or lead" were deported without trial. Germany at least carried through on its constitution, but, as finally adopted, this gave very little power to the people. Radicals were hounded from the country.

Not until fourteen years later, in 1862, was German Social

Democracy officially born when a brilliant young man, Ferdinand Lassalle, addressed an artisans' association in Berlin. His economic interpretation of history and his idea that the workers represented the class of the future were Marxian, but his objective was different. He rejected revolution, wishing only to help the human race toward freedom by way of universal suffrage. Lassalle was arrested as a result of his speech. The publicity made for more invitations to lecture, and, by 1863, the Universal German Workingmen's Association was created. As its leader Lassalle's political future seemed assured.

Then fate intervened romantically. He became engaged to one Fräulein von Dönniges, and her father, as clearly conscious of class differences as was the young swain, pushed his daughter in the direction of Prince von Racowitza. If the dispute had been resolved verbally, Lassalle might have won, but, hotheadedly, he offered a challenge to a duel. The prince, better versed in marksmanship than debate, readily accepted, and on August 28, 1864, Lassalle's careers, both romantic and political, came to an abrupt end.

His successor in the German association, Bernhard Becker, entitled himself "President of Mankind," but he was misunderstood, generally disliked for his pomposities, and did nothing to advance the cause of social democracy. The Franco-Prussian War further weakened its development. A subsequent depression swelled the Social Democratic Workingmen's party (officially so designated in 1875) to a membership of half a million and gave the party twelve members in the Reichstag.

While Ferdinand Lassalle had led the first splintering off from Marxism at mid-century, another vigorous leader, Eduard Bernstein, was soon to champion a further defection. Born a Berliner in 1850, Bernstein was torn between his friendship with Friedrich Engels on one hand and the British Fabians on the other. In the end, he chose the Fabian way and called for a revision of Marxist philosophy. He denied the imminent collapse of capitalism and urged that the workingman had better prospects through democratic political involvement than through revolution. Like the Fabians, he denied any "final aim" and sought a wider base for his theories than Marxian economics. This was pure democratic socialism. The Communists branded it revisionism, a term later applied to anyone deviating from official Soviet views.

State Socialism Bernstein was not the only German "Fabian." A group of university professors advocated a slow evolution of social conditions along Fabian lines. Owing to its academic setting, this system became known as "Socialism of the Chair." Though responsible indirectly for many social reforms, it also indirectly had a disruptive effect upon the course of social democracy in Germany. The "Herr Professor Doktor" has always been accorded unusual respect in that country, and one of the respecters was Germany's "iron chancellor," Bismarck. Under academic influence, Bismarck undertook a program of state socialism that did nothing to reconstruct the social order but did mitigate many evils of capitalism. Bismarck was no humanitarian. He did not love his workingmen, but he knew a nation could not be sound if its society was weak and its people discontented. For the sake of a militarily strong state, he instituted government ownership of certain utilities and put through social insurance and old-age security for the worker. Here, without benefit of a name, the welfare state was born. It would influence liberal Englishmen and a reform-minded Teddy Roosevelt in the United States. It would in some ways foreshadow Franklin D. Roosevelt's New Deal; but in imperial Germany such concessions from the top would spill the wind from the sails of the Social Democrats, who moved for reform from the depths. It would also strengthen Germany, as Bismarck had wished, for a war he neither contemplated or lived to see.

Meanwhile, the German Social Democratic party struggled along under the leadership of August Bebel without the benefit of Bismarck or any direct help from the professors who, unlike the English Fabians, held themselves aloof from the street. Bebel had lived with abject poverty and was the embodiment of working-class revolt. He refused to support his country in the Franco-Prussian War of 1870–71, for he saw the hope of the future in the proposed Paris Commune. Such attitudes incurred the hostility of Chancellor Bismarck, who attacked the party by suppression on the one hand and reforms from the top on the other. Typically, World War I caused a party split, some members rallying to the colors, others regarding the war as a capitalist betrayal of workingmen everywhere. With defeat, the old rulers were gone. More nationalistic parties were humiliated. Not so the Social Democrats, who had never favored military glory. They saw their mission as that of healing the unjust wounds of an imperialist war.

A decade of chaos ensued in Germany, with many parties competing, some Fascist, others Communist. In the middle, the Social Democrats rose to a majority in 1928 and shouldered the burdens of the unpopular Versailles peace treaty. A year of comparative economic stability followed, and the party set about attempting to administer capitalism in a quite unsocialistic manner. Then came the Great Depression, and the rise of NASDAP (National-Socialist-German-Workers-Party), more commonly known as the Nazi party, professing to be all things to all men. Of course, once the party had gained political control, both business and labor fell under its unbending direction. It brought socialism in the sense of state management of business, but there was nothing democratic about it. Purely fascistic and dictatorial, it quickly brought about the fall of the Social Democrats, along with every other party in Hitler's new German Reich.

The Social Democrats were out of business from 1933 until 1945, when the party was reorganized in the ashes of

World War II under the leadership of Kurt Schumacher. Schumacher, who had lost one arm in World War I, was a Socialist editor between wars, and a concentration-camp inmate under the Nazis. His objective was to extend the party's appeal to the middle class and to various religious groups. A leg amputation in 1948 led indirectly to Schumacher's death in 1952, and the Social Democratic party leadership shifted to the increasingly popular mayor of West Berlin, Willy Brandt. Brandt was an early Socialist who had fled the Nazis to Norway, where he studied at the University of Oslo. Later he became a journalist in Spain, and during the war he supported the resistance movement from Sweden. However until the retirement in 1963 of the dynamic Christian Democratic chancellor, Konrad Adenauer, Brandt and his party made little progress.

Thereafter Brandt began to gain national influence and in 1969 took over as chancellor in the first major power shift since the war. Though an avowed Socialist, Brandt achieved power in too affluent a period to effect profound changes. Germany was no longer war-ravaged and grateful for any sort of change, but a prospering capitalist nation with the soundest economy in Europe. Private industry was simply too big and healthy for Brandt to consider nationalizing it and, apart from minor welfare reforms, he has done little to rock this treasure-laden vessel.

Austria Linked to Germany geographically as it has often been politically is Austria. One of Austria's earliest experiments with socialism was that of Karl Lueger (1844–1910). His Christian Socialist party imagined labor problems being solved by the setting-up of church-administered cooperative enterprises. Of greater impact politically up through the First World War was Dr. Viktor Adler, leader of the Austrian Social Democratic party, and his son Friedrich, its militant party secretary. While the elder Adler believed the Socialist party must focus its attention on the Austrian proletariat, his son held out for the unity of the workers of the world. The former view prevailed overwhelmingly, although the Socialists took a united stand against the war when it came. In 1916, when Premier Count Stürgkh refused to attend a conference for the purpose of restoring constitutional government, Friedrich Adler expressed his displeasure by shooting the premier dead. Though condemned to death, Adler was released from prison at the war's end.

In 1919, the Socialists became the strongest party in the Austrian National Assembly. Its chancellor, Karl Renner, put through a democratic constitution and adopted sweeping reforms, only to give way gradually to the Christian Socialists. Meanwhile local fascism was on the rise, and it was supported by a private army, big business, and the Catholic church. Fear of the new menace restored life to the Social Democrats, but it was too late. Dr. Engelbert Dollfuss, former secretary of agriculture in Lower Austria and the new chancellor, gave vent to totalitarian notions of his own. He began ruling by decree. A devout Catholic, he had little use for Socialists and began making their political life uncomfortable, particularly in so-called Red Vienna. Socialist workers were ordered to join the "Patriotic Front," a substitute for all parties in what Dollfuss conceived as a Christian corporate state following Italian lines. Civil war was inevitable, and it came early in 1934. Ill-armed, the Socialists could hold out for only four days, and their leaders were hanged or driven into exile. They remained powerless until the end of World War II, when a coalition government was set up under the People's party, the Socialists, and the Communists. In 1946 this resulted in the nationalization of the oil, shipping, and metallurgical industries, along with electric power and banking. The following year it became clear that Austria favored the Western allies, and the Communists resigned from the coalition. It carried on, with the Socialists supplying the president of the republic and the People's party furnishing the chancellor. In 1966, the Social Democratic party was reduced to the government's chief opposition party, but it regained its majority in 1970.

Italian and Spanish Socialism   Italian socialism started with church sanction. Pope Leo XIII, in his 1891 Encyclical "Rerum Novarum," censured the evils of the industrial age and spoke of the inhumanity of employers and the unbridled greed of competition. Until the First World War, the Socialists in Italy enjoyed increasing strength. They opposed the war vigorously, none more than the editor of the Socialist newspaper *Avanti,* one Benito Mussolini. The war was to change him, as it was to change socialism throughout the continent.

During the war, Mussolini began to drift from the socialistic posture of resistance into support for what he had at first called the "Bourgeois War." In consequence, he was expelled from the Socialist party, which was itself changing and fracturing as a large part of its membership was drawn toward communism. These factions for a while were too busy to notice Mussolini and his new fascism. Founded in 1919, the Fascist party seemed merely to outdemand the Socialist in terms of reform. Not until 1921 did Mussolini begin his swing toward the Right, at which time he began to see the Socialist programs as dangerous. By 1924, he had so rigged elections in favor of his Fascists that, when Socialist deputy Giacomo Matteotti protested, he was murdered within days. The killers got off with serving two-month sentences as Mussolini loudly assumed full responsibility for the Matteotti Affair and characterized the incident as an expression of the magnificent passion of the best youth of Italy. From then on, socialism was driven underground.

In 1931, Pope Pius XI lamented the concentration of industrial power in his encyclical "Quadragesimo Anno" but this echo of Pope Leo's message was drowned out by Mussolini's own publication *The Doctrine of Fascism*. This statement denounced democratic government and advocated a power elite, namely himself, and a one-party state. Economically, Italian labor and business were to be divided into guilds, each with a theoretical monopoly in its field. The anticipated efficiency of this system would be galvanized for the nation's good as a whole, which, according to fascism, meant violent chauvinism and inevitable wars of expansion.

Mussolini's war of expansion, World War II, left Italy among the vanquished, and her self-styled Caesar was hung up by the heels. Fascism was out. Unfortunately for the now respectable Socialists, they were too much embroiled in their own quarrels to fill the vacuum. While the Communist party was strong and appealing, the Socialist party faltered under the leadership of Pietro Nenni. In 1952 Nenni had received the Stalin Peace Prize, largely for resisting Italy's membership in NATO, and he did not know whether to turn East or West. Not until Russia crushed the Hungarian Revolution in 1956 did he make up his mind and cut back on political cooperation with the Communists. This flirtation with communism had led to the splintering off of a Democratic Socialist group. Its connections with the established Socialist party have been influenced by Italy's mercurial relationship with the Communists ever since.

Despite close links to Mussolini, Spanish fascism survived the Second World War because its dictator, General Franco, adroitly managed to avoid military involvement with his former partner in liquidating Spanish socialism. Spain has always been susceptible to political adventure, and socialism was launched there in 1879 with the Social Labor party. It was only one among many struggling protest groups, and it received impetus from World War I as did the nations more deeply involved.

Between the world wars, labor agitation had forced the king from his throne and replaced him with a provisional republican government, which set out briskly on a leftist course, proposing to nationalize all big estates, businesses, and the Catholic church. Needless to say, the landed aristocracy, both temporal and clerical, were horrified when a coalition of parties—the Republican Left, Socialist, Republican Union, Communist, Trotskyite, Syndicalist, and Anarchist—won the election of 1936. The fascistically conservative army was promptly called on to protect the establishment. War raged for three bitter years, with leftists and rightists from all over Europe tuning up for the greater struggle to come. Fascism prevailed, and socialism, along with other dissident groups, has remained underground.

Throughout the rest of western Europe, nineteenth-century industrialization produced its labor class and a political response along Socialist lines. The first party formed was Switzerland's Grütli Union, originally established as a progressive party in 1838, and favoring socialism after 1878. A Dutch Social Democratic Union also arrived in 1878, broke with the anarchist element in 1894, and was largely instrumental in preserving Holland's neutrality during the First World War. A Belgian Labor party was born in 1885. In general, these parties grew in strength until the First World War, which they resisted. Patriotic sentiment tended to weaken them, and only with the war's end and a general awareness of its mindless horror did they make further gains in the interwar period.

Remote in her mountain fastness, Switzerland was affected only indirectly by the two wars. Socialism continued its slow growth there. By 1935, the party had gained fifty seats in the lower house as against two for the Communists. Switzerland had never been a setting for extremists, and when Hitler began to arm near her borders, the Socialists, though dedicated in principle to pacifism, worked along with the government to strengthen national defenses.

Postwar European Socialism Holland and Belgium were among World War II's innocent victims. Political reaction favored the Socialists, and when Queen Wilhelmina returned to Holland, Willem Schermerhorn, a Socialist, a former resistance leader, and a university professor, became premier. Even as Britain saw a counterreaction after the first postwar years, so in Holland the Catholic People's party has reasserted itself and the Socialists have at best found themselves part of a coalition government.

The same pattern occurred in Belgium. With the peace, Belgium was ready for changes, and Paul-Henri Spaak became the head of a Socialist government in 1947. An attorney, son of a poet, a playwright, and Belgium foreign minister in exile during the war, Spaak favored strong international cooperation, becoming known as "Mr. Europe." He also managed to put through universal suffrage and a treaty for mutual aid among the Benelux countries. Subsequently the Socialists gave way to a more conservative government, but they continue to share occasionally in coalitions.

Scandinavia Geographically set apart from the rest of western Europe is Scandinavia. From the violent Viking days the area has settled through centuries of active history into countries with a balanced social structure unknown in the rest of Europe. Without political convulsions, a unique brand of welfare-state socialism has had the chance to develop. "A home for the people" can be taken as Sweden's motto, and welfare programs reflecting a similar philosophy exist in Denmark and Norway. The goal is not simply to cure distress in such fashion as giving financial aid to hard-pressed mothers. Rather it is to prevent hardship. In Denmark cash is given to every mother for each child under eighteen regardless of family circumstances. Sweden offers free health supervision for all, preventive medicine for infants, free transportation to vacation camps when needed, and free college tuition. Mothers receive maternity leave from their jobs with two-thirds pay and free confinement care. All Swedes belong to a government-run health insurance plan, and pensions are granted at the rate of two-thirds of the working wage plus cost-of-living payments.

Thirteen percent of the national income, as opposed to 6 percent in the United States, is devoted to welfare.

Since 1809 Sweden has existed under a stable constitutional democracy with the king subject to his ministers and obliged, as in Great Britain, to choose the prime minister and cabinet from that party that holds the majority in the Riksdag, or Parliament. The Swedish Social Democratic party was organized in 1889. Hjalmar Branting became the party leader in 1907 and later the first Socialist prime minister. Entering into a coalition cabinet at the inception of World War I, he opposed Swedish participation in the war. The Social Democrats gained temporary control of the government in the 1920s. Aided by the depression, it settled in to stay in 1932. Strengthened by its success in overcoming unemployment, the Social Democrats have been in office ever since, with Conservatives, Liberals, and a Center party in cooperative opposition.

This quiet acceptance of social democracy has made for a profound difference in the application of socialism as contrasted with Great Britain, where Labour has always been an embattled, in-and-out-of-power party. With the Conservatives in militant opposition in Great Britain, Labour has had to resort to a rigid, hard-to-reverse program of nationalization of prime industries. Sweden, on the other hand, having no such need to burn bridges, has worked out a far more flexible program of government supervision and cooperation with essentially independent business and industry.

In Norway the early Labor party, at first called the Social Democratic party, worked closely with communism. It favored disarmament during World War I and the Russian revolution drew many of its members to the Left. However a coalition of Democratic Socialists with other groups won fifty-nine seats in the Storting, Norway's one-chamber legislature, and the following year, as the Labor party, they were asked to form a government. The first Socialist premier, Christian Hornsrud, called for a bill redistributing wealth, and he was immediately attacked as trying to Bolshevize Norway. Socialism fell into brief disfavor, and communism lost its one remaining seat in the government.

Conservative rule was brief, however. In 1932, thanks in part to the depression, Johan Nygaardsvold, a former railroad worker in the United States, became premier. In the name of Labor, he launched a public-works program, old-age pension law, unemployment insurance, and a form of a state industrial bank. By this time, Norwegian Socialists had severed all ties with Russian communism.

Unlike Sweden, Norway was invaded during World War II by Nazi Germany. The Labor party endorsed a valiant but hopeless resistance, and during the occupation Major Vidkun Quisling served as puppet prime minister, giving his name to a new kind of traitor. With the war's end, the Laborites obtained their first absolute majority in Parliament under the leadership of Einar Gerhardsen, who had spent four years in a Nazi prison. Like the other European countries actively involved in World War II, Socialist Labor success came as a reaction. Not until 1965 was there a swing back to the Right, and this a mild one under which the four non-Socialist parties—Conservative, Center, Christian People's, and Liberal—formed a coalition. Scandals in the Ministry of Industry were in part responsible for their combined success, and, though Labor remained the biggest single party, it had lost its absolute majority and freedom of action. Again in 1969, the four-party coalition was voted into office.

The Socialist movement arrived early in Denmark; perhaps too early, for in 1872 the police dispersed the first large Socialist meeting there, and the chief of police was able to assure the minister of justice that the menace of socialism had been terminated in Denmark. Six years later, however, the Social Democratic party was formed. Not so radical as the early Socialists, the party grew steadily in power and influence until, following the close of World War I, by 1924 it had fifty-five representatives in the Folketing. This was ten more than its nearest competitor, the Farmers' party. Though moderate in objectives, the Socialists did move for public ownership of the central bank, the major insurance companies, and certain monopolized industries. When asked to make common cause with the Communists against Nazi Germany, they refused, saying there was no virtue in fighting one dictatorship only to clear the way for another. Either way they were lost, and in April, 1940, the Nazis occupied Denmark with the excuse that Denmark's own military force was inadequate to protect it against Allied attempts to overthrow its democracy. During the war, Denmark was just one more Nazi province; better off than most, perhaps, as very little fighting or destruction took place. With the war's end, the government was in a position to resume operations, and a Scandinavian welfare state has been the result.

Social Democracy in Finland, often considered part of Scandinavia, was launched by the establishment of *Tyomies* ("The Workers"), a Socialist newspaper, in 1895. A Labor party was formed four years later. At that time, Finland was dominated by the Russian czar. But when he tried to draft Finnish soldiers into the Russian army, they went on strike. The Bolshevik upheaval in Russia saw the czardom swept away. Turmoil in Finland was just beginning. The Social Democrats took over and, heady with success, cast their lot with the Communist Red Guards. They promptly lost out to the German army, which, in 1918, elected a German prince king of Finland. A month later, Germany went down to defeat and labor began to reorganize in Finland. By 1926, a Socialist government was established, bringing with it old-age pensions and health insurance.

However, bitterness against the Communists, who were busily burrowing into the trade-union movement, was brought to a head by their antireligious demonstrations at Lapua, a center of right-wing Lutheran opposition in Finland. A vigilante group, calling themselves the Lapuans, arose to expel the demonstrators. The response was sufficient to crush the Communists and drive the Socialists from office for the next decade. Just before World War II, the Socialists had again become the largest of the eight parties represented in Parliament, and it has since participated in those welfare reforms common to all Scandinavian countries.

The usual Scandinavian stereotype pictures a healthy, blond, humorless people, fond of sex, skiing, cheese, dry-heat baths, and hard liquor. They are opposed to violence except in the form of suicide, which has probably been induced by a staggering burden of taxation. Such generalizations are never accurate, but it is possible to speak of a Scandinavian approach to economics and welfare.

In this respect, Sweden has been the pioneer, achieving the world's first Socialist government by democratic means in 1920. In terms of welfare, parents receive over $200 dollars upon the birth of a child, and almost $200 a year for his maintenance until he reaches the age of sixteen. His vitamins, vaccinations, and all medical care are free, as is his schooling, which includes meals and books. When it comes time for him to find a job, free employment service is available, along with unemployment insurance and free legal aid. Low-cost loans are obtainable when he wants to build a house. He receives a pension upon retirement sufficient to let him lead the life to which he has grown accustomed, and when he dies his burial is free. To eradicate the demeaning image of welfare, so-called social supermarkets have been established to offer service, not charity. Encouraged in the notion that, since he has paid stiff taxes, such services are due and owing, the "client" is free there to seek out legal, psychiatric, medical, or financial help with little or no stigma attached.

While the immediate goal of the Social Democrats was to nationalize industry, the Industrial Revolution had come late enough in Scandinavia for Socialists to benefit from the mistakes of others. To date, only about 6 percent of Swedish industry has been nationalized. Instead of state ownership has come strong state control. In addition to heavy taxation, minimum-working-age laws, and special courts to consider labor-management disputes, the government keeps all business, and particularly that business relating to national interest, under close scrutiny. No business can survive long without governmental approval, and the result is that government, employers' organizations, and trade unions remain in close contact and achieve compromise decisions when it comes to general policies and the allocating of profits. Realizing that the individual might otherwise have no recourse against such a strong central government, the office of ombudsman has been created. This person is a citizen's representative, a lawyer appointed by Parliament to receive and hear individuals' complaints against the government. When cause is indicated, he has the power to investigate any governmental office for evidence of misbehavior.

Finally, one Socialist invention is particularly strong throughout Scandinavia, and that is the cooperative movement. Borrowed intact from the Rochdale weavers of Britain, 95 percent of Denmark's farmers are members of cooperatives for purposes that vary from buying seed and selling pigs to utilizing co-op slaughterhouses and borrowing from co-op banks. In Norway cooperatives began with the fishermen, who needed to expedite their catch on the way to market. In Sweden the single largest industrial organization is Ko-operativa Forbundet, with over a million members.

Scandinavia, more than any other place on earth, has had the chance to experiment soberly and peacefully with socialism. There is little want in those countries, and little inclination to return to more competitive ways. Poverty, overcrowding, population explosion are all under relatively good control. Critics have said that total welfare has destroyed motivation and blunted ambition. Perhaps. Perhaps the success of Scandinavian socialism is a function of unique circumstances, even ethnic temperament, that cannot be transported. With most businesses privately owned, some might argue that what they have is not socialism at all, but welfarism. No matter: whatever they do have works well enough in an imperfect world and provides the clearest example of evolving democratic socialism in a situation relatively free of external or internal violence.

Middle Eastern Socialism

Among the divergent peoples of the Levant, much attention is given to socialism. Exploited by colonial powers, disputed for its strategic location, there is no older community than Egypt, where the doctrine of Arab socialism was recently announced amid the pangs of rebirth into a nationhood of the twentieth century. Across the Sinai Peninsula lies Israel, a young nation in a hard land, surrounded on three sides by hostile neighbors. There unique forms of socialism have developed, not so much as theory but as natural adaptation for survival's sake.

The Kibbutzim To the nonresident Turks and Persians the arrival of Jewish settlers around 1900 seemed an opportunity to sell off totally useless plots of desert or malarial marshland. One such unappetizing swamp was known as the "death spot." The new arrivals bought it eagerly and named it Degania after the small blue cornflowers of the countryside. Despite Turkish expectation, this and other unlikely Jewish communities began to thrive and spread from the energetic efforts of the young settlers. Most small farming communities would have been defeated by the harsh environment, but the kibbutzim developed by the new settlers, who practiced a kind of militant Fourierism, were ideally suited to the struggle.

The settlers, in the first instance healthy young men and women, live a communal life. There is no private property, no money. Meals are taken communally, and even the raising of children is done by the group, with occasional visits by the children to their parents. These communities are run by a democratically elected executive committee whose major decisions are subject to group approval. A dissatisfied member may depart at any time, but the prospect of going virtually naked into the world is a definite deterrent. Should a member desire special treatment, such as time and funds to study at a university outside the kibbutz complex, his request is set before the executive committee, which will furnish funds from the common treasury if they are available and if it deems the request appropriate. Tasks are assigned by the works committee, and anyone legitimately unfit to work through illness, accident, or old age is cared for by the community.

This is democratic socialism to delight many a utopian philosopher. There are those who would say it is an austere and unnatural way of life, and under other less warlike circumstances they might well be right, but circumstances in Palestine, now Israel, have never been ideal. The land is unyielding. Only with industrialization and heavy equipment has the struggle with nature moved toward victory. The contest with the surrounding Arab world is no more resolved than it ever was. It has simply magnified so that each kibbutz is no longer alone against its Arab neighbors but is rather a link in a chain of outpost fortresses forming a kind of Maginot Line to keep out the enemy. This is particularly true of those kibbutzim that occupy border and strategic locations. They are the front line of defense, and the continued need for physical security, the sense of belonging, against a threatening world, have perpetuated a unique form of socialism.

In the interior and toward the coast where there is no direct menace from local Arabs, where communities can rely more on the army than upon themselves for protection, the tendency is for community living to be modified. These so-called moshavim are settlements made up of cooperative small landholders. Each member owns his own house and farms his own land, but purchasing is done jointly, as is the marketing of produce and the renting of heavy equipment. Today the moshavim are more numerous than the kibbutzim, and the trend seems likely to continue.

The State of Israel   Half a century after the invention of the kibbutz, Israel became a nation. Westward-looking, with a population primarily of European stock, a democratic system was established along Franco-English lines. Universal suffrage begins at the age of eighteen, and each party, of which there are several—more than the tribes of old—receives proportional representation in the Knesset. Voting is not for candidates but for the particular party and its philosophy, with a choice throughout the spectrum from Left to Right: Communist, Anti-Zionist, Israeli. In the center is Mapai, rather like Britain's Labour party, which, during its formative years, was led by David Ben-Gurion. Nearly twenty years before nationhood, Mapai existed with the objective of blending national and socialist aspirations toward the rebuilding of the ancient Jewish homeland. To this end its early efforts were to encourage migration and a return to the soil with collective and cooperative settlements.

After Israel declared its statehood, Mapai headed the provisional government with Ben-Gurion as prime minister. He was succeeded in 1963 by his finance minister, Levi Eshkol. In 1969 the Mapai, Rafi, and Achdut Avoda parties merged into one powerful Israel Labor party under the prime ministership of Golda Meir. Domestically, Mrs. Meir has continued to support the Socialist traditions of her party. Toward the Arabs her position has been unyielding, with none of the pacifism that has been part of democratic socialism in theory, if seldom in practice.

Unique in its scope is Israel's General Federation of Labor. Histadrut, as it is called, has over a million members, over half the nation's adult population and 90 percent of her wage earners. The size of Histadrut has made it a state within a state. Many depend on it for its free clinics and hospitals, its schools teaching advanced Hebrew, its newspaper, and its sports organization. Though private investment still flourishes in Israel, Histadrut's enterprises alone account for 25 percent of Israel's national income. As prime supporter of the Labor party, its urgings have led to governmental control of the water supply and to education and labor exchanges, a state of political affairs that has caused Histadrut's enemies to refer to its headquarters in Tel Aviv as "the Kremlin."

Despite such criticisms, democratic socialism has worked well in Israel. The rigors of this young country's international situation might seem to demand a more totalitarian regime, but at its core Israel's governmental elite is comprised of well-educated Europeans accustomed to democratic ways and painfully aware of the potential for persecution inherent in such totalitarian systems as Nazi Germany and Soviet Russia.

Arab Socialism The case is quite the contrary among Israel's Arab neighbors, where the twentieth-century theme of first importance has been nationalism. The second, heard particularly from Nasser's Egypt, is socialism. Centuries of authoritarian rule made for a backward and politically docile people. When the British withdrew from Egypt after the Second World War, leaving a decadent government in the equally decadent and incompetent hands of King Farouk, an upheaval was inevitable. It is only remarkable that the change came as smoothly as it did. Grotesquely overweight, devoted to food and pornography, the king lost his last army support when it became public knowledge that during the Palestine war Cairo profiteers had deliberately supplied the Egyptian army with defective arms and ammunition. The army was disgusted, particularly a clique of free officers led by Gamal Abdel Nasser and Mohammed Naguib. They achieved Farouk's bloodless ouster in the summer of 1952, and Naguib became Egypt's first president.

Presently Nasser's greater intelligence and more radical temperament was Naguib's undoing. In 1954 he had to resign, and with undeniable dedication Nasser set about modernizing his new state, which in 1958 became the United Arab Republic, for a while including Syria. The process to be followed was entitled Arab socialism. It was more democratic in theory than in practice, where methods showed adept schooling in fascism. Pluralistic government was rapidly abandoned on the grounds that the Egyptian people lacked political maturity and the parties would maneuver for shortsighted and selfish goals and not for true national interests. Similar semantics have been voiced by other totalitarian governments but, in Egypt's case, there is much truth in the statements. Until the twentieth century most Arab countries were governed by royal or colonial decisions. The people lack background in political responsibility. Likewise, the industrial setting that produced Western-style capitalism and the subsequent socialistic reaction were absent in these agrarian countries.

Fortunately for most Egyptians, Nasser was a sincere and gifted leader with a deep love for his poor people. For their benefit, he accepted the Marxian notion of a political revolution, but he could not endure the Marxian dogma of class struggle. It went against his conviction that Egypt was basically one great family with oppression coming from outside imperialism rather than from a capitalist class within. To prepare the political scene, Nasser's officers were gradually installed in the ministries of Egypt's vast bureaucratic system. The press was controlled and parties such as the disruptive Muslim Brotherhood were suppressed, so that by 1955 there remained but one decision-making center: Nasser and his military associates, operating nominally through an assembly that had the power only to advise. Lest this advice at times prove embarrassing, candidates with inadequate ideas were screened out.

With the safe suppression of anarchy, along with democracy, Arab socialism was ready to move into high gear. In the interests of growth and an equitable distribution of income, the first goal was to destroy the "monopoly capitalists" and distribute the income to end exploitation. This process was met with less popular resistance than it might have been elsewhere, for much of the capital attacked was in the possession of foreigners or minority groups of Greeks and Jews. First to be nationalized were the major factories and the Suez Canal. Then the laws of 1961 nationalized the remaining banks and insurance companies and almost all industry needed for planning. This left private enterprise dominant only in handicrafts, retail trades, and personal services. While some wholesale and export trades still remain privately owned, they have been placed under rigid state controls.

Arab socialism has evolved with little theory and no dogma apart from the goal of a fair distribution of wealth. Necessity, not reasoned conviction, has dictated policy. The benefits have often gone to the few rather than to the many, as in the case of the nationalization of foreign enterprises, which created new employment only with the displacement of foreigners. Also, a rapidly expanding population and excessive defense spending have tended to mask and diminish progress.

The Egyptian Experience Prior to 1952, Egypt's national economy was dominated by agriculture, which furnished more than 80 percent of exports and which was largely controlled by foreign interests. The traditional method was for a wealthy absentee landlord clique to rent out farmland, usually through a rental agent who took his cut from the land-hungry masses. The result, for the peasant farmer, or fellah, was bare and grubbing subsistence. After 1952, a reformed land-tenure system was established, which drastically cut the size of estate holdings and redistributed much land among the actual tillers of the soil. These small units were joined into larger cooperatives. Subsequently individual landholdings were again reduced, and foreigners were prohibited from owning any land whatsoever. The result is that the peasant owns his land, but in practical fact he must cooperate with adjacent small landholders in raising one single crop for the sake of overall productivity and ease of marketing. Crop rotation is enforced, and the physical well-being, if not the independence, of the peasant has shown improvement.

Arab socialism is too young to be fairly judged. It is unlikely that democratic socialism could have been implemented from the beginning for lack of political and economic development. A sincere effort to better the lot of the Egyptian peasant and worker has been made against the obstacles of overpopulation, ignorance, inertia, endemic disease, and constant military defeats by Israel. Whether Arab socialism freezes into a totalitarian bureaucratic mold or, with the improvement of living conditions and general education, moves toward a more democratic system remains for the future and for Anwar Sadat, who succeeded to the presidency of the United Arab Republic upon Nasser's death in 1970, to determine.

Socialism in Africa

In Africa during the last twenty-five years skyscraper cities have sprouted from the jungle. The old ways are dying and modernization is spreading through the vast continent. A new black Africa is being born, but it would be wrong to suppose that in blackness alone there is the making of unity any more than "whiteness" has unified western Europe. There is rivalry and distance and distinct tribal codes that fence off one group from another socially. Yet among the leadership, at least, there is a sense of "blackness" or of "Negritude," as Léopold Senghor, the Socialist president of Senegal, described it. This awareness of a black African community has come as the result of white Western exploitation, the cruelest example of which was the slave trade, which saw some sixty million Africans kidnapped to the Western Hemisphere. Not even the passage of a century can blot out such a memory or the other results of European exploitation and colonization.

Not until post–World War II Britain, under Socialist urging, denounced its imperial ways did the big change begin.

1960 was the feverish year of independence, so much desired, so long awaited that the new black African leadership was caught short. Like the man who tries to batter down a locked door only to have it spring open, many stumbled and fell flat or stood there in amazement, never having pondered beyond the conquest of the door itself.

Foreign Influences Advice and persuasion were abundantly available. The old colonial powers, particularly Great Britain, France, and Belgium, wanted to retain good relations and had left behind at least the hint of their own systems of government. The Soviet Union and Red China have sought disciples for communism. This competitive wooing by world powers has put the new black African states in a tempting if dangerous position. By and large they are poor countries, wanting rapid economic growth. They are grateful for aid and assistance and not particularly concerned with what political label is affixed. They are aware of these labels, however, and in general have rejected them. Western capitalism represents a slow and expensive development. Besides, it has a nasty taste reminiscent of the old days of exploitation. Marxist communism, like capitalism, is based solely on materialism, and, though its more rapid development is seductive, its totalitarian foreignness has not been entirely overlooked. Between the two is socialism, which offers rapid economic planning along with the sense of freedom developed in western Europe where most of the able black Africans have been educated.

In theory, at least, black Africa has chosen socialism. The result of adapting an ideology that is the product of a complex, industrial, Christian, class-oriented society to an essentially agrarian, totemistic, tribal structure is bound to be unique. Of fundamental concern is to what extent the results will be democratic. On the one hand, power cliques have tried to nationalize the economy purely for selfish reasons of power

and enrichment. On the other, a sincere effort to adapt socialism to the black African setting has been undertaken.

Léopold Senghor of Senegal   Chief spokesman and theorist behind African socialism is President Léopold Sédar Senghor of Senegal. Raised a Catholic among some two dozen
brothers and sisters, Senghor early demonstrated his own
singular abilities, received a fine education at the Sorbonne in
France, and subsequently taught in French secondary schools.
Developing a strong sense of Negritude, he spent much of
his time translating American Negro poetry. In 1959 Senghor,
in his pleas for independence, spoke of grafting European socialism on the old roots of Negro-African communalism. On
the one hand, he disavowed the complete laissez-faire of capitalism; on the other, he rejected total nationalization of the
economy. He described the Marxian dogma of the ''dictatorship of the proletariat'' as a gargling formula.

African Socialism   What Africa needed first, in Senghor's
opinion, was cultural independence and a freedom of choice,
which he foresaw as leading to a form of West African humanism. Unlike Russia or western Europe, there did not exist
the class groupings that had been responsible for capitalism
and communism. There was virtually no proletariat of wage-
earning workers, but rather a sense of native African collectiv-
ism inherent in tribalism that emphasized the fulfillment of the
group above the individual. As Senghor saw it, the European
strove to distinguish himself from his fellows while the African
preferred to live within his tribe or emerging nation. To remain
in harmony with other men, animals, nature in general, and
God: these are lofty ideals that Senghor has tried to implement. The object of African socialism is man in his totality, not
simply economic man.

In Senegal, this classlessness is more fact than theory, for
in the European sense there is no proletariat of workers, no

business bourgeoisie, no capitalists, not even any real capital to nationalize. Though in Senegal there may be no class tensions, there are tribal groups with differing, even hostile interests. For harmony's sake, the chiefdoms must be suppressed whenever possible. This was allegedly not to achieve a one-party system, which has been advocated by some African Socialists, for Senghor felt a single party represented the danger of government by clique. He did, however, favor a party of the masses to be led by intellectuals, who would be the people's conscience and guide them from their fog of animal needs toward political consciousness.

Economically, Senghor favored scientific planning for growth. When it seemed appropriate, there would be nationalization, but he saw that merely as one pragmatic means among many. For reasons of human solidarity and political strategy, he has confidently and with good reason expected a flow of ready capital from western Europe, the United States, and the Communist countries. So as not to kill the geese that thus far have continued laying golden eggs, he has disclaimed the nationalization of capital in general. Most of it is foreign investment, and such an act would cause loss of credit and perhaps lead to major conflict.

Speaking generally, the major elements of African socialism in practice include a network of agricultural cooperatives and publicly initiated village industry. State governments have tended to assume ownership of major national projects such as irrigation, electricity, and transportation. There has been careful supervision of all major industries in the interest of an overall economic plan that emphasizes the rapid expansion of employment, housing, and public health.

Kenya Such has been the case in Kenya. Since receiving its independence, this country has pursued a policy of African socialism under its first and only prime minister, Jomo Kenyatta. Born into the dominant Kikuyu tribe, Kenyatta was educated at the Church of Scotland mission school and spent fifteen years in England and Europe. He was particularly inspired by the Jamaican Negro Marcus Garvey, who raised funds for a great black fleet to reverse the drift of the slave trade and originated the motto "Wake Up, Africa." Always pushing for independence, Kenyatta was imprisoned for involvement in the Mau Mau terror. He emerged as a martyr and messiah to his tribe. When independence came, he was swept into the prime minister's chair virtually by acclamation. The only opposition came from the African Democratic Union party, led by Ronald Ngala, which subsequently joined with Kenyatta in a one-party state.

Negritude is, of course, a central theme. It has led Kenyatta, a trained anthropologist, to such excesses as the encouragement of savage tribal rights including the clitoridectomy of young girls simply on the basis of its being customary. On the plus side, his popularity and Kenya's general stability have led to a doubling in secondary school enrollment, much progress in terms of public health, extensive road development, and a rapidly growing tourist business. Foreign confidence has been sufficient for substantial investment, and a mixed economy has been achieved with both public and private ownership. An awareness that nationalization of business will cut down on private and foreign investment has tended to limit public ownership to areas with clearly attainable and necessary social objectives.

Kenya has its socialism, but one wonders to what extent it will ever have democracy under its one-party system. Kenyatta has called for complete adult participation in politics, and this may make for the same sort of representation as one finds in the inherently democratic tribal structure, a democracy that is not, however, geared to the abounding concerns of a modern state. In a 1965 White Paper, the late Tom Mboya, Kenyatta's talented minister of economic planning and development, declared that one-party socialism would preserve constructive criticism along democratic lines, a position justified by the absence of conflicting class interests. Tribal enmity, however, undeniably does exist in Kenya and other black African republics, and it was tribal enmity that, ironically, was responsible for Mboya's assassination in the summer of 1969. Kenyatta continues as the wise and grand old man. Under him, one-party socialism flourishes, along with democracy, in spirit if not in concrete fact. But his most promising disciple is now dead, and there is no one of Kenyatta's magnetism waiting in the wings. Kenya's political and economic future depend on the changeover.

Black Africa seems inevitably committed to the ideology of "African socialism." How it works out in practice depends on the vagaries of present and future leadership. The indications are that socialism will exist in a mixed economy much as has been the case in Britain, the Scandinavian countries, and other nations following this pragmatic ideology. A restraint on excessive nationalization is the need for foreign investment, vital to the development of countries lacking in both funds and industry. Such aid is not likely to be accepted with strings attached. With the memory of a colonial past, a satellite future is contemplated by no African leaders, whether their inclinations are totalitarian or democratic. Once foreign aid is no longer a major restraint, it may well be that the young black African nations will mature into representative and democratic systems. Philibert Tsiranana, president of the Malagasy Republic and head of its ruling Social Democratic party, is trying to stimulate a genuine opposition party. His efforts appear to be sincere and may well be emulated. If so, African socialism may develop along truly democratic lines.

The Far East and the Pacific

India is the great melting pot of man: Aryans, Greeks, Huns, Turks, Afghans. It is the birthplace of many religions: Buddhism, Sikhism, Jainism. It is also the scene of a remarkable twentieth-century experiment. There a new nation is struggling to emerge without force or violence into the modern industrial age. Where socialism has been imposed upon a fully developed industrial economy, as in most Western nations, a democratic framework has proved effective. Underdeveloped countries lacking a democratic tradition and unaccustomed to democratic self-government have normally drifted toward authoritarianism. Nowhere are the problems of change more complex or on a vaster scale than in India, which makes her experiment with democratic socialism the most significant ever undertaken.

With the collapse of the Mogul Empire in the beginning of the eighteenth century, the Indian peninsula was ripe for apportionment among princelings and Western colonizers. Britain ruled the seas. The vast East India Company under the supervision of Lord Clive of Plassey excluded most Portuguese, Dutch, and French exploiters by the mid-eighteenth century. The crown did not take over from the East India Company until 1858, the year after the Indian Mutiny. Hindu and Moslem soldiers rose in revolt when the rumor went around that new cartridges shipped out from England for use in their muskets had been packed in the fat of pigs—detested by Muslims—and of cows—sacred to the Hindus. Some historians consider this abortive revolt as the beginning of the Indian independence movement. If so, the British were not aware of it. For them, India was nothing but a cotton field for the Manchester mills. The natives were kept illiterate. Industry was discouraged, for Britain wanted the twofold benefit of obtaining the raw material and then selling it back as finished products.

Indian Independence The twentieth century brought its wars and the breaking away of colonial nations. India's liberation was only a matter of time. It was fortunate for both Britain and India that the latter's growing sense of nationalism was kept in bounds by two great leaders, the late Prime Minister Nehru and his mentor, Mahatma Gandhi. Nehru was a trained lawyer, more worldly than Gandhi, and he accepted Fabian socialism as a guide. He believed in Britain's mixed economy, which left room for private enterprise as long as it did not waste production on luxury goods. Gandhi was a different sort of Socialist. He did not favor state ownership, for he did not trust a concentration of political power. Instead he preferred self-sufficient and self-educated villagers, guided by representative councils with a minimum of government from above. This democratic and agrarian socialism was to be achieved by nonviolent revolution, and it was this method rather than the results achieved that proved Gandhi's great service to humanity.

When independence finally came in 1947, India was left with a British system of administration and communication, and a nationalist movement split between Gandhi's decentralization and Nehru's industrialization, sponsored and planned by a national government. The saintly Gandhi was to die, forgiving his assassin even as the fatal bullets tore into him. Nehru was to live on as prime minister.

With the end of the Second World War, the pressure for independence had been threatening an explosion. Great Britain's Conservative prime minister, Winston Churchill, who had just led his empire to victory, held out, saying, ''I was not appointed His Majesty's Prime Minister to preside over the liquidation of the British Empire.'' Clement Attlee, the incoming Labour party leader, felt otherwise, and it has been said that nothing became Britain in India so much as the manner of her departing. Independence came peacefully, though subsequent riots between Hindus and Moslems were to leave thousands dead. This basically religious rivalry has left far more bitterness than British colonialism, which did bestow certain advantages: new political ideas and institutions, a representative government and a liberal tradition, a functioning bureaucracy, and, in the arts, an appreciation for the Indian past as well as for new Western forms such as the novel and the drama. More important, under the British, a new mercantile economy had evolved. It produced a business middle class that tended to disinherit the older nobility. The landed aristocracy, with its distrust of the masses, had been bypassed in the twentieth century and took no part in the cultural renaissance.

Under the new federal republic, India was divided into twenty-seven states, which were later reduced to seventeen states and eleven territories. Federal and state governments were granted concurrent powers in economic and social planning, although the state powers were very limited. Over all, Prime Minister Nehru's Congress party emerged as the dominant force. It was not the only Socialist party. There were the older Praja Socialist group and the Congress Socialist party, which in 1952 (after Gandhi's death), broke away from the

Congress party, whose goals of equitable distribution of wealth it regarded as too conservative. In the first elections the opposition was not large or well organized, though it has remained free and vigorous. Voters, many illiterate, voted with enthusiasm and reasonable understanding of local issues. Two hundred thousand voting stations were required for this biggest of all free elections. To cope with the illiteracy problem, ballot boxes had to be marked with the symbols of the major parties, such as two bullocks for the Congress party, a thatched house for the Praja Socialists, a sickle and an ear of corn for the Communists.

Since its first victory the Congress party has continued in power, sometimes uneasily and with a gradual tendency to favor the growing strength of the federal government at the expense of the states. The only basis for state government at all had been regional rivalries. This negative foundation, coupled with the surviving spirit of Gandhi in the strong village governments, has discouraged the development of state administrations. Growing border problems with Pakistan and China called for a vigorous central government, based on the British parliamentary model. To it was added a United States-type of Supreme Court, which, unlike the courts in the British system, could challenge the acts of Parliament.

Socialism in India Actually, India's problems had begun long before Western exploitation with the arrival of the East India Company. Even at that early date, the population explosion was already out of hand. Then, as today, government planning was vital. Economic planning at the federal level was the key to Nehru's government. There was no other recourse if a functioning modern economy was to be achieved. This is true of most emergent nations. Traditionally, Western capitalism has stood for a freely operating economy. For the government to involve itself is to restrict the freedom of private enterprise. For the free-enterprise system to work, however, requires consumers with money to buy the goods that are produced. Where the bulk of the population exists, as in India, at a bare subsistence level, there are no consumers with funds to buy. With nothing being sold, there is no reason to invest and free enterprise never gets off the ground. A planned economy, particularly with access to aid from wealthy countries, has some hope of breaking this hopeless cycle, a task made more difficult by a constantly growing population. As yet, efforts at encouraging birth control in India have not had much success. Results in other areas have been more encouraging.

Government planning along British lines has become almost a religion, for if it fails, democratic India will fail. Planning, on a five-year basis, involves a national planning commission that sets investment targets. In the nationalized sector of the economy are strategic and heavy industries, railways, airlines, life insurance, and central banking. In the private sector, voluntary cooperation is sought and usually achieved between business and government.

The first great question was whether to concentrate on almost nonexistent industry, following the Russian model for long-term growth, or to deal primarily with agriculture, for food was desperately needed. The latter course was more humane but susceptible to less conspicuous results. Nonetheless, agriculture became the focus of India's first five-year plan. Available land was distributed in small parcels to the peasants. While it was worked separately, however, poor results were achieved, so cooperatives were encouraged.

Under a totalitarian regime, land would simply have been seized from the rich. In Russia or Red China, the problem might have been dealt with by the purge of thousands of landlords. From India's poor but democratic government, compensation was required, but it was hard to finance. Where land was freely given, it was usually of poor quality. Nevertheless, a variety of modestly successful expedients have been attempted. New fertilizers and improved seeds and insecticides have been introduced. Local moneylenders exacting as much as 40 percent interest have been an Indian village institution that has kept the small farmer in constant debt. Moneylenders have been curbed by a new cooperative state bank. To further encourage cooperation and community projects and to instill a sense of urgency into its people, the government has sent out educated representatives trained in rural extension work. In the villages, these instructors have introduced new techniques, conducted field demonstrations, led group discussions, and aroused interest with audiovisual teaching. They have achieved the construction of new latrines and schools, with government funds advanced to boost such projects. Ideally, this teaching will develop a thirst for betterment and for education, but the hurdles to overcome are many and high. Enthusiasm can last only so long. Peasants are conservative and fear change. Funds are limited. Old beliefs such as the attitude toward cows are difficult to overcome. Hungry people refuse to eat their hungry cows, saving what grain there is for these 180 million sacred beasts, and seed merchants stand by while their meager cribs are pillaged by armies of sacred monkeys.

The Five-Year Plans Nevertheless, progress was made during the first five-year plan. The key to any successful agriculture system is dependable water. About 20 percent of all cultivated land in India, some 90 million acres, raises what is called "rain-fed rice." This rice depended in the past, and to a large extent still does, on the four-month period of the monsoon. If the rain did not come, the crop withered and died. If it came too generously, the crop and a good many farmers were washed away. To stabilize this dependence on weather, a vast irrigation project was initiated by the government, with major dams at Hirakud, Bhakra-Nangal, and other key places. An additional 14 million acres were put under cultivation.

The first five-year plan seemed a qualified success. The

people were eating more regularly. National expenditures, which had been drained away on the importation of food, could be allocated to industrial projects, chemical plants, and heavy industry, particularly steel production, which became the focus of the second five-year plan. Without steel, home industry could not grow, and India was rich in untapped iron ore. Foreign aid was sought and received, primarily from the Soviet Union. In February of 1959, the first blast furnace began to roar at the mud-hut village of Bhilai. Villagers and officials wept for joy. Poems were published about the mystery of red-hot iron. Other plants began functioning at Durgapur and Rourkela. India was up and running.

India's third and fourth five-year plans, however, have had rough sledding. Industrial progress has been slower and more costly than had been expected. Some officials wanted to scrap the plans entirely for the sake of ad hoc economic measures. Others saw steel being paid for by starvation, a theme that the failure of the monsoon rains in the mid-1960s emphasized. Consequently, while continuing to make progress, the third and fourth five-year plans have been devoted to making good on the unfulfilled goals of the earlier two.

Methods have become more pragmatic and nationalization of business, so central to the English example, has been limited to the most vital industries. Agriculture has remained entirely in the private sector, as has most production, particularly the smaller, less strategic producers such as tool and bicycle manufacturers. However, the government has established the right to inspect and assign priorities. All businesses are subject to intervention along Scandinavian lines if they are suspected of operating contrary to the common good or of unfairly amassing wealth. On some occasions, as with the Sindri Fertilizer Corporation, the government has first established a business and then sold it to private owners, while retaining the right of supervision. In general, this pragmatic approach has shown favorable results, with a growing accord between owner and government. The latter, in return for cooperation, has granted financial assistance, tax concessions, and tariff protection.

Democratic socialism in India faces massive problems. Many have been overcome but more lie ahead. Domestically there is a growing population of the poor and ignorant. On her borders there are the brooding presence of Red China and an always hostile Pakistan against whom a bitter war was fought in 1971. Yet the Indian government is basically stable and the people satisfied that reasonable effort is being made in their behalf which seems to offer democratic socialism time to test itself. It is hoped that the wishes expressed by Prime Minister Indira Gandhi will be eventually fulfilled: "What we all want is a better life, with more food, employment, and opportunity in conditions of economic justice, equality, and with individual freedom."

Burma   Other Far Eastern areas subject at one time or another to British influence have tried socialism as a governmental system. Burma, a battleground during the Second World War, had formerly been dominated by foreign capital. As a result, in the 1930s a strong and militant Socialist party had sprung up and been ruthlessly suppressed. Students subsequently formed the Dobama Assi-a-yong party, which represented left-wing anti-imperialism. During the war one section of the party organized itself into a Burmese revolutionary party, and a hard core, the "Thirty Comrades," trained in Japan and fought with the Japanese against the British. The harsh reality of the Japanese occupation proved disillusioning, and in the end an Anti-Fascist Peoples' Freedom League aided the British toward their final victory in 1945. It was this AFPFL that formed a Socialist government under Premier Aung San the following year.

Democratic ambitions in Burma were high for nationalizing industry, such as it was, as well as for forming cooperatives in agriculture. Unhappily, by the late 1950s the party had split into hostile factions. From the turmoil General Ne Win emerged as a totalitarian Socialist strong man who arrested his political opponents. After forming the Burmese Socialist Program party, he moved quickly to nationalize banks, foreign trade, wholesale trade, mining, newspapers, and private schools. General Ne Win remains chairman of the revolutionary council and prime minister. He has nationalized virtually the entire Burmese economy, leading the country into a centralized, despotic form of socialism, in which democratic processes have been abandoned. Burma provides a good example of what can happen to democratic socialism when applied in a country unprepared economically or politically for its natural growth.

New Zealand   Socialism has had a far calmer course in New Zealand, that isolated Norway of the South Pacific untroubled by wars or domestic upheaval. Three major political parties exist in New Zealand's Parliament of some eighty seats. Two, the Social Credit party and the Liberal Rightist party, are minor. Today the National party, led by Prime Minister Keith Holyoake, is in power and has been for the last twelve years despite a strong Labour challenge.

New Zealand was colonized largely in the nineteenth century by dissident English farmers and workers who were disturbed with British capitalism and filled with Socialist ideas. It was natural for a Labour party to be launched in the 1880s. Within ten years, a Liberal-Labour Alliance had taken over the government under the leadership of Richard Seddon, a former coal miner from Lancashire. Before the turn of the century, labor relations acts had been passed to protect workers, and legal machinery was developed to establish minimum wages. Large estates were subdivided, and aid was given to small farmers. The first old-age pension act in the English-speaking world became law in New Zealand. By the 1930s, the Labour party absorbed the liberal wing and continued to enact advanced social and economic measures. Among them were the forty-hour week and, in 1938, a social-security act with health and medical benefits.

As in Scandinavia, the goal achieved in New Zealand was social security from the cradle to the grave, with free schooling until nineteen years of age, many government grants to university students, and pensions for those over sixty years of age. Weekly benefits went to the unemployed and a free health service was available to all. A levy on wages has provided all the required funds, with the result being a near equality of real income. Welfare benefits are sufficient to eliminate poverty in the nation, while high taxes have put a ceiling on earnings and muffled incentive. There are few rich men, and this limiting of a man's economic potential has caused a brain drain of the most able. They have departed, leaving New Zealand a paradise for the average man and a haven for the distressed.

In 1949, because of the war strain on the budget and the shortage of consumer goods, New Zealand's Labour party was defeated by the National party. Labour returned to power in 1957 but soon lost out again to the Nationalists, who were supported by farmers, industry, and a wealthy urban coalition. Despite Labour's loss of power, the state still controls the economy. The state intervenes in insurance and transport, and it owns most electrical installations, coal mines, and forest reserves. To avoid labor-versus-management friction, a 1954 act forbids strikes and lockouts and furnishes a court of arbitration whose decisions are binding.

Although the National party has done little to advance the course of socialism in New Zealand, it has done virtually nothing to counteract measures already instituted, for politics in this peaceful island chain are low-keyed and the positions of the two major parties are not far apart. The labor leaders are more middle-class, more British, and less trade-union-oriented than is the case with neighboring Australia.

Australia   Like New Zealand, Australia is basically a capitalist democracy, but with a great deal of socialistic state intervention in business and daily affairs and with a particularly strong trade-union and labor influence making itself felt in economic relations. Like the United States, Australia has a constitution and a Federal High Court as final arbiter. The democratic process is encouraged by placing a $4.50 fine on failure to vote in elections of members of federal and state parliaments. The manner of vote tabulation is proportional, meaning that each citizen votes his order of preference among the available candidates. Then the candidate with the least number of votes has his ballots distributed proportionately among his rivals until one remains with a majority of primary and preferential votes. Such a system gives even minor parties tactical strength, and Australian politicking has been a bitter and hard-fought process over the years.

Representing the conservative urban middle class is the Liberal party, and it has often formed a powerful coalition with the rural Country party under the shrewd and sometimes ruthless leadership of Sir Robert Gordon Menzies. The Communist party, though small, has at times wielded power in the trade unions. In the late 1940s it conspired to take over the unions entirely. A reaction led by Roman Catholic activists under Bartholomew Santamaria crushed the Communist party and weakened Australia's formerly strong Labour party. Labour was split between the traditional Australian Labour party and Santamaria's splinter group. Consequently the coalition of the Democratic Labour, Liberal, and Country parties has held narrow sway for the last twenty years.

But labor has had its day in Australia, and may well do so again. It has left an indelible mark. Trade unions were already campaigning for shorter hours, higher pay, and the elimination of competition for jobs from cheap imported Chinese labor when, in 1885, William Lane began printing *The Boomerang,* a Socialist paper. Lane was a cultured Englishman who tried to move the trade unions toward socialism. This meant political involvement, but labor resisted politics until after 1890, when a strike of sheepherders, shearers, shipworkers, and others was broken up by the government. Thereafter, a Labour party under Socialist guidance spread from New South Wales into the other Australian states and before World War I held a majority in the legislatures of four states. In the 1920s the party introduced state insurance, as it contested control of the government with the Liberals. An early Labour prime minister, Andrew Fisher, created the Commonwealth Bank, and, later, coal mines, some butcher shops, and even restaurants and hotels became state-owned. Never so solidly entrenched as in New Zealand, Labour reached a zenith of power late in World War II and has since been on the decline. As is characteristic of Socialist legislation worldwide, however, once enacted it has been taken for granted and not repealed.

Japan   Japan, where post–World War II capitalism has become a near religion, has never had direct links with British socialism and only distant and interrupted contact with the world movement. Yet the ideology's fortunes in Japan have closely responded to its reception throughout the world. The movement had a modest beginning in 1897 when Professor Sen Katayama began teaching socialism and trade unionism at the university level. Within two years, students had formed a Socialist League in Tokyo. Two years later, a party emerged, only to be dissolved by the police. World War I brought Japan its first industrial boom and a corresponding growth in labor strength. Unions and strikes were grudgingly allowed. Not until 1925 was universal manhood suffrage granted, and eleven years later the unified Social Masses party elected eighteen members to the Diet, or Parliament. But the timing was by no means auspicious. Militarism was on the rise, and presently the army extended its power to form a totalitarian corporate state. Political parties were dissolved and did not appear again until Imperial Japan lay in ruins after World War II.

The old ruling class was decimated by the war and the Socialist party came into the open once more, forming in 1945 the Social Democratic party with Tetsu Katayama as its chairman. Its platform was political freedom, democracy, and the rejection of capitalism and war, all very acceptable to a war-benumbed and desolated land. Aided by this wave of reaction and by the first results of woman suffrage, the Socialists won over 90 of the 466 seats in the Diet. By 1947, they had become the largest party, with 143 seats, and Katayama was prime minister. Socialism had reached flood tide in Japan, as it had in Britain and the rest of the world. The labor movement was briefly encouraged. Cultivated lands were transferred from landlord to tenant farmer, but bitter party controversies were in the making, with stresses left and right. The end of the United States military occupation in 1952 led to bloody riots, and the country was ready for a conservative return. Capitalism began to surge ahead full throttle, though the Socialists briefly unified their attack against the building of a new army. This Socialist gathering of resistance was diminished in 1959 with the breaking off of a right-wing Democratic Socialist party. Socialists of every stamp have been in divided opposition in Japan ever since.

North America

The Western Hemisphere has not been neglected by socialism, though it has had no easy time there. Starting with Canada, one might expect to find an Australia or a New Zealand of
the North, for there is a widespread element of the frontier as
well as the British background. But as a frontier, Canada is
old; and the British background is pre-Socialist. Then, too,
there is Canada's close economic dependence on the United
States, which remains the world's foremost bastion of capitalistic free enterprise.

Socialists in Canada A Socialist Labor party started
around the turn of the century, but with few results, as it took
the First World War to provide Canada with an industrial base.
Several labor parties emerged there after the conflict and,
moving toward unity, elected James Shaver Woodsworth to
Parliament. Combining the talents of divinity student, school-
teacher, minister, labor leader, longshoreman, and pacifist,
Woodsworth led the movement into the midst of World War II.

The party made progress, particularly in Western Canada, and from 1944 to 1964 the only Socialist state government in North America flourished in Saskatchewan.

American Socialism   Socialism had its early American advocates. Horace Greeley, editor of *The New York Tribune,* found socialism compatible with the cause of abolition. Through his paper, he extended the idea of slavery to include "that condition in which one human being exists mainly as a convenience for other human beings." He wanted to see the ownership of wealth in the hands of the laborer rather than the early capitalist.

The most famous utopian experiment in the United States began as a purely American venture and involved such noted New England intellectuals as Ralph Waldo Emerson and Nathaniel Hawthorne. It began in 1840 when a Unitarian minister, George Ripley, bought a two-hundred-acre milk farm near West Roxbury, Massachusetts. His plan was to substitute a system of brotherly cooperation for selfish competition. In his small community the members were to work a set number of hours and receive uniform compensation, as well as free support for children, the old, and the sick. Unfortunately the community's character changed with the importation of French Fourierism and the changing of the project's name to the Brook Farm Phalanstery. Disputes arose at the same time as a new unitary phalanstery building was nearing completion. When an accidental fire burned the building to the ground insufficient enthusiasm remained for rebuilding and Brook Farm came to an end in 1847. Longer-lasting was the North American Phalanstery at Red Bank, New Jersey, but it, too, died before the Civil War. Robert Owen, who had no success with his ideal community in Scotland, exported a group of Owenites to New Harmony, Indiana, where it briefly flourished.

Social upheaval and revolution in the countries of Europe, particularly in Germany, expelled a number of Socialist revolutionaries to American shores in the early 1850s. The Civil War preempted growing social tensions, but it also furnished more fertile soil for them with the vast spread of industry. In 1876, a coalition of laborite parties at a convention in Philadelphia gave birth to a Workingmen's party committed to Socialist principles. Later this group would split, for the times were restless and the group mingled Communist-Socialist tendencies, the former favoring economic action, the latter political.

There was also an urban-versus-rural rivalry within the party. Foreign-born Daniel De Leon led the eastern urban Socialist Labor party. In the Midwest, Indiana-born Eugene Victor Debs was jailed in 1894 for his involvement in the vast Pullman strike. The workers had refused to work the railroad cars if the company would not arbitrate. President Cleveland had dispatched troops, and Debs, a liberal, went to jail for six months, guilty of contempt of court. He had entered jail a Democrat. There he brooded, read widely, and emerged a Socialist, to drive crowds wild with such battle cries as "We've been cursed with the reign of gold long enough!"

The two branches of late-nineteenth-century socialism would never get together again. De Leon could not poll a third of the votes gained by Debs, and he saw Debs's efforts as a purely utopian attempt to revise the economy. At least Debs offered grass-roots American socialism, and, with the backing of such popular writers as Jack London and Upton Sinclair, he would run five times for the presidency. He achieved a modest, though increasing following up until the First World War, involvement in which the party actively resisted. This stand would return Debs to jail and cause the suppression of the Socialist press.

Politically, socialism in the United States had passed its peak. The end of World War I saw a drift to the Communist Left. Party membership slumped, though Debs kept running through the election of 1920. With Debs's passing in 1926, Norman Thomas took up the Socialist baton. Thomas was born a

Presbyterian in Marion, Ohio, and was valedictorian at Princeton in 1905. Studying for the ministry, he became a pastor in East Harlem, New York. He ran for the presidency six times, beginning in 1928 when the Socialists polled a quarter of a million votes. Four years later, the depression raised that total to nearly a million, but it also ushered in Roosevelt's New Deal, which supplanted much of socialism's appeal for twenty years. Then, in 1948, Henry Wallace came out of the prairie, bringing with him the ghosts of Franklin D. Roosevelt and William Jennings Bryan. The keynote of his revitalized Progressive party was "Wallace or War." Vast nationalization of basic industries was promised, sufficient to bring the American Communist party into coalition.

Unhappy with what seemed to him the Progressive party's political irresponsibility, Thomas ran again on the official Socialist ticket. In the election, Wallace was buried and Thomas was entombed beneath him. That was Norman Thomas's last campaign. The clear rejection led to reappraisals that dictated socialism's approach thereafter. No longer would the party waste its resources on humiliating and inevitable political defeat, nor would it espouse the Communist way of boring subversively from within. Like the Fabians of old, they would promote the ideas of diffused public ownership with economic power being placed in the hands of voluntary associations rather than under sovereign authority, ideas that in substance are very much along Scandinavian lines.

Why has socialism in the United States, off to a promising start before World War I, failed so utterly? While the two wars boosted British socialism to the front, they seem to have had quite the opposite effect in the United States. This is not surprising, since Britain's world power was diminished by the wars while the power of the United States was enhanced. Economically, Britain was near collapse after the last great war, and many of her businesses might have failed but for governmental intervention. Business in the United States was never better than during that period. While Great Britain has always been used to concentrated government—the king in former times, the prime minister and Parliament today—not only is federal power in the United States divided between various departments, but there is the state-versus-federal rivalry, and nationalization always raises the fear of big central government as it never has in Britain.

The labor unions in the United States have never proved receptive to political involvement. Their approach has remained economic and within the capitalistic system. The intellectual-political consciousness of the Fabian Society in Britain, which moved the unions into politics, hardly existed in the United States. Then, too, the very nature of a political campaign in the United States makes the rise of an effective third party unlikely and prohibitively expensive. The voter, though perhaps preferring the platform of a minority candidate, will seldom throw his vote away. As a practical matter he is more likely to vote for that major party candidate who seems the least unsatisfactory.

Changing Economic Realities Finally, there is the undeniable fact that socialism, though it remains an unpopular concept in the United States, has seen many of its short-term goals achieved there. This process began with the trust-busting period of the early twentieth century and picked up speed during the Great Depression of the 1930s, when the country became disillusioned with laissez-faire capitalism and the Democratic party initiated the New Deal. The National Labor Relations Act, the Agricultural Adjustment Act, and stepped-up progressive taxation all made for government intervention in free enterprise. Although neither a Republican nor a Democratic President would wisely speak of nationalizing the economy, the depression measures followed by the demands of a wartime economy turned the government into industry's biggest customer. The two have been mutually dependent ever since.

A clear example was that of Lockheed Aircraft, which, upon the impending cancellation of government contracts, threatened to close down, thereby throwing thousands of men out of work. To avoid such hardship, the contracts were retained and a substantial loan was granted. Many other industries have been subsidized in the national interest. Most recently, for the purpose of controlling runaway inflation, a Republican administration instituted national wage and price controls, a drastic measure heretofore limited to wartime. This is not nationalization of business and industry, but it is not entirely free enterprise, either. Other "socializing" measures are likely in the future, such as a national medical insurance program that smacks of Britain's very successful socialized medicine.

Under this new concept of the welfare state, with its tendency toward socialism, capitalism has been preserved while many of the ills that have nourished outright socialism in other lands have been cured. It remains a little-known fact that a black citizen of the United States has a greater statistical chance of a college education than a white citizen of Great Britain, West Germany, France, or Italy. He is apt to live better and earn more than the average European, though within the United States, in relation to the white population, his opportunities for higher education and a good job lag unconscionably far behind.

The Socialist party, like the Communist, is old-hat now and generates little excitement in the United States. It has been ignored by the brash New Left, a multiplicity of young and idealistic groups pursuing civil liberties, peace, and the equal rights of women. They resent the "establishment," rely on direct action, and in general achieve little. Socialists have given them support for their good intentions on the one hand.

On the other, they have deplored their lack of consistent pro-grams, their failure to realize the importance of organized labor, and their total scorn for earlier, better-thought-out ef-forts to achieve reform.

Socialism in Latin America and the Caribbean

The Latin American countries are numerous, but they share more with each other in terms of background and culture than do the countries of the world's other great land masses. The Indians were there first, with systems both primitive and highly civilized. Then the Spanish and Portuguese destroyed the more highly developed Indian cultures for gold and the greater glory of God. The less-advanced tribes were left to their jungles and mountain peaks. Along with the superimposed ways of Southern Europe arrived a vast infusion of black slaves from Africa during the eighteenth and early nineteenth centuries. During this period, Spain and Portugal were passing into an international eclipse, torn at home and abroad by the Napoleonic wars and held back economically by a conservative church, ineffectual government, and the failure to develop industry.

Throughout the first half of the nineteenth century, liberty came to one South American country after another. With victory and independence came high hopes. The principles of the young United States were to be followed. Grass-roots democracy had come, or so it was briefly hoped, but even Simón Bolívar, the George Washington of South America, became just one more of South America's strong men as soon as he undertook the tedious business of governing the newly independent nation of Venezuela. He abolished the constitution, became an absolute dictator, and finally fled from assassins. The pattern was to be repeated by others in Venezuela and throughout South America.

In support of this tyrannical establishment was the wealthy, powerful, and conservative church, and a clique of Spanish and Portuguese aristocrats who regarded the peasant masses no differently than they had done under colonial administration. Together, they had the economic strength to support private armies. However, as war became more technical with the industrial age, private armies gave way to professionalism. After 1900, the generals began moving indirectly, or, as has been more typical, as a quiet force in the background, leaving the government alone as long as it conducts the country's affairs in relative tranquillity and without diminishing military expenditures.

Meanwhile, the rural peasant population made up of native Indians, former black slaves, the poorer Spanish, and mixtures of all three lived in squalor and ignorance. To them, virtual serfs in the past, twentieth-century industrialization brought hope of urban prosperity. An increasing flow of unskilled labor left the countryside and formed squatters' shantytowns in the growing cities. Most of these people remained undernourished, illiterate, and unproductive, with a high birthrate and few prospects other than those offered by radical new social ideas. Among those that appeared, South American socialism came to full flower between the two world wars.

In Brazil, a party shift toward communism caused the Socialists to be declared illegal in 1927. Active political participation has never been encouraged there. Government, even reform government, has been a military matter. One country, however, where socialism found receptive soil was Chile. A Socialist Labor party, formed in 1912, moved first toward communism, then veered to the right, until, in 1932, a new junta proclaimed Chile a Socialist republic. For twelve days it urged, among other reforms, drastic taxation on big incomes, and then it was ousted. The following turmoil resulted in a military coup, subsequent leftist coalitions and schisms, with the whole moving toward socialistic reform. In 1964, Salvador Allende, a Marxist-Socialist, ran for president against Eduardo Frei, a Christian Democrat with socialistic ideas. Frei won that election, but in the next election, in 1971, Allende became the first elected Marxist president, an event that properly belongs, and is discussed in the volume on *Communism*.

In short, socialism has made a recent mark throughout South America. It would be tedious to describe the rise and fall of countless leaders, the success or failure of all their programs. Instead, the example set by three of these countries, Peru, Venezuela, and Argentina, should provide adequate material for consideration, since the economic and social problems are much the same throughout the continent.

Peru's Apra In Peru, during the period between the major world wars, a new political party was born under the watchful eye of a military junta. It was grandiosely entitled Alianza Popular Revolucionaria Americana, and more modestly referred to as Apra. Its founder, Víctor Raúl Haya de la Torre, had cut his radical teeth during the brooding dictatorship of Augusto Leguía, and Haya's firebrand statements to the effect that land and industry should be nationalized had caused his deportation in 1923. Regardless of his views, Haya formed no alliance with Peruvian Communists for he saw more danger in them than in American imperialism. When he finally returned to Lima, Haya began lecturing on peasant cooperatives. The people loved the thick-set, hawk-nosed little man who had spent most of his life in prison or on the run, and consequently it was not long until a down-at-the-heels mansion in Lima became a revered place. Called the Casa del Pueblo, it was both political headquarters and shrine, filled with Haya's pictures, books, even the bars from the prison cell where he had been incarcerated.

At the Casa, lectures were held and gratis instruction given in such far-flung subjects as music and barbering. A hard-up peasant could get anything from a free meal to medical attention or a haircut there. Within five years, Apra was the strongest political party in Peru, and in 1931 Haya seemed to have won the presidential election. It was not to be, then, or ever. Cohorts of an army-backed candidate, Colonel Luis M. Sánchez Cerro, tallied up the vote and blandly declared their colonel the winner. Five years later, Apra won in the general election. A disturbed military forced Congress to suspend the vote tabulation, and the former president's term was extended.

Apra was understandably frustrated, and its continuing campaigns for civil liberties often turned violent. An assassination was going too far, and the party leadership went into exile. The party itself was declared illegal. Sympathetic to Apra's vibrations, however, the government instituted minor reforms in the late thirties, including worker housing, a social security law, and free public school breakfasts. Meanwhile, Apra began to modify its preachments, encouraging capitalistic development of industry and in general trying to soften more radical, peasant-oriented policies in order to satisfy a growing middle class.

The end of World War II saw scholarly President José Luis Bustamante presiding over modest social reform in Peru. An idealist, he wished to share the administration with an apparently matured Apra party. He was not counting on its new clique of "Young Turks," who began to infiltrate the government, making use of strong-arm squads and finally of assassination, until Peru was in a state of virtual revolution. Unable to cope, Bustamente occupied himself in writing esoteric legal theses until, in the time-honored manner, General Manuel Odría crushed Apra and took charge. He ruled until 1956 by which time social unrest seemed to be encouraging a resurgence of Apra, and General Perez Godoy rolled his tank over the gates of the National Palace. This new strong man, wiser and more forgiving than most, held the reins until 1963 when he too was supplanted via a general election by Fernando Belaúnde. Belaúnde instituted a program of moderate reform with the help of an updated approach by the Catholic church in Peru, which has pioneered in efforts to furnish tools, seeds, and livestock, on a cooperative basis, while preaching reform to the selfish rich. Meanwhile, Belaúnde undertook road construction, community-development projects, and a democratization of the army.

In 1964, an agrarian reform law was presented to correct an imbalance that left 80 percent of the nation's arable land in the hands of less than 2 percent of the population. This new distribution excludes lands that have been worked for the nation's good. The program was timely, and it tended to forestall land-grabbing. Land-hungry Indians had begun marching onto big estates with knives and "liberating" them forcibly with shouts of "Long live the peasant's union!" In the city, barriadas, or shantytowns, were forming around industrial centers. The squatters resisted all police efforts to evict them. They formed their own schools and village councils, and the enormity of the problem was such that the government had to give in and provide legal means for the squatters to obtain title to the land. In such ways does social change take place.

Only, Apra has passed its prime. Its leadership is old without ever having enjoyed the fruits of the elections that it so often won. Yet Apra has been a moving force in Peru, and there is much truth in the party saying, "First they said we were mad. Then they said we were Communists, and now they say, 'What's all the fuss? It's exactly what we had in mind all the time.' "

More recently, the president of Peru, Major General Juan Velasco Alvarado, has taken socialism a step forward with the nationalization of a United States oil company, a subsidiary of Standard Oil. Communications and water sources have also been nationalized, and large landholdings continue to be expropriated for Indian use. Whether this military socialism will move into more or less democratic and representative processes in Peru and in other Latin American countries only the future will tell. All that is certain is that change of a dramatic nature is inevitable.

Appropriate to the temper of Peru and perhaps to all of Latin America is the Indian festival tradition of binding a condor to a bull's back and then releasing the pair into the crowd of would-be matadors. The bull, which once represented Spain, now more fittingly represents the wealthy aristocracy. The condor has always been the symbol of the natives, and it tears at the bull, who takes out after the crowd. Once the bull becomes exhausted, the bird is detached and given strong beer to drink. Then, if it can still fly, it is a good omen. The native has triumphed. This symbolic ritual takes place among the poor, in their mountains, in their slums, in Cuzco, the Indian capital. The wealthy are in bustling Lima, or on their plantations. Change, more or less orderly, is in progress in Peru, and among its neighbors. The question is, will it take place fast enough to avoid violent upheaval?

Venezuela Following its liberation from Spain, Venezuela was torn by years of political upheaval until Antonio Guzmán Blanco seized power in 1869. Other dictators followed, the most durable of whom was Juan Vicente Goméz. In charge from 1908 until his death, a natural one, in 1935, Goméz did meet Venezuela's external debts but in the process he eliminated the last traces of constitutional government, running the country virtually as a private family business. Thanks to the proceeds from the country's vast oil reserves, roads and railroads were built creating a facade of public wealth. Yet the people were poor under Goméz and his successor and their dissatisfaction was given expression by numerous exiled students who began preaching a range of revolutionary doctrines from communism to fascism. The most gifted of these young prophets was Romulo Betancourt, who had absorbed Karl Marx.

Betancourt believed in the division of big estates and in distribution of land to the poor. In exile, he had helped found the Communist party of Costa Rica. Returning to Venezuela, he initiated the Acción Democrática, a party less radical than the Communists but still favoring land distribution. In 1945, riding an army coup, he became president. He ruled by decree, but, unlike his predecessors, he did not let the taste of power overcome his principles. He put through a new law for universal suffrage as well as for the direct election of the president (formerly the Congress had controlled this election). Vested interests opposed such modernization, and the wealthy, supported by the Roman Catholic clergy, pressured the army into ousting Betancourt and his hand-picked successor, Rómulo Gallegos, a noted author.

The dictatorship of Pérez Jiménez followed. It was the usual gold-braid affair, and it lasted five years. A military revolt sent the reactionary little dictator first into plush exile in the Dominican Republic and finally to jail. Betancourt returned to the country with the goodwill of his people and international well-wishers. Unfortunately he inherited a land with severe economic problems. As president again, he began by cutting back on grandiose public building. He concentrated instead on basic industry, steel, and electricity, while leaving secondary industry to private enterprise. Foreign investment was encouraged as long as it was not monopolistic and against national interest. Action has been undertaken in terms of land distribution, and new cooperative settlements have been begun for the sake of pooling scarce heavy machinery. This middle-of-the-road socialism of course attracted enemies, both from the conservative Right and from the Communist Left, and terrorism has for the last several years remained a fact of life in Venezuela.

In 1963, Betancourt retired in favor of Raúl Leoni as his successor. Leoni in turn was replaced, five years later, by Rafael Caldera, who is backed by a strong army more detached from aristocratic influence than it used to be. The potentially rich economy has begun to prosper. Altogether, the prospects seem bright of its countering the growth of a poor and frustrated urban population.

Argentina Unique to Latin America as well as to the world was socialism as it developed in the fascist context of Argentina. Socialism was introduced early by Esteban Echeverría, who returned from France after the abortive revolution of 1848. Marxism became strong through the century though well contained by the government, which operated under a constitution of 1853 modeled after the United States Constitution. Actual power was concentrated in the president, who in turn looked to the army for support.

Another power center was organized labor, and in 1896 Juan B. Justo launched the Socialist Labor party. Splits occurred during the twenties, first with a Communist faction and then with a more nationalistic Independent Socialist party. All party strife ended with World War II, and General Pedro P. Ramírez, the minister of war, led a coup d'etat with the support of the army and the friendly Axis powers. Ramírez was an admirer of European fascism. Though he had promised constitutionality, within a week of his taking office it became apparent that he would fail to keep his word, and a younger, more homogeneous "colonels" clique began to identify itself with the masses.

Juan Perón Its eventual leader was Juan Perón. Like Mussolini, Perón imagined himself a "Macho" (he-man), and despite his oddly short arms, he was a creditable swordsman. His father had been a sheep-raiser, his mother a Spanish Creole. In 1939 he visited Italy, where he noted il Duce's successes, as well as his serious mistake of allying himself with a dominating power, Germany. He also studied the results of the Spanish Civil War and saw the desolation that resulted from allowing antagonism to develop between socialistic labor and a fascistic army, a tendency that already existed in Argentina. Returning there, Perón rode along with the military government, and in 1943 he took over the department of labor and social security. He quickly won labor over by allowing unions to strike and to elect their own officials, as long as the officials were partial to Perón. Within three years, Perón and his devoted following of workers, known as the shirtless ones, had even the military cowed. Hired thugs helped to ensure his election as president in 1946 for a six-year term. The year before, he had married a woman even more remarkable than himself.

Eva Duarte, at twenty-five, was half Perón's age. A party girl and second-rate actress when she first met Perón, she popularized his labor programs during the 1945 days of crisis. Born to the masses, her sympathy was genuine, and she was involved until her death in Peronist charities. A servile Congress bestowed on her the title "Spiritual Chief of the Nation," while at the same time naming Perón "Liberator of the Republic."

Perón's high tide came in the next few years with a frantic blend of socialism and fascism. He nationalized the central bank, took over privately owned grain elevators and universities, stocked the Supreme Court with picked men, bought up and nationalized the British-owned railroad network, revised the Constitution to allow a president to be indefinitely reelected, and changed the name of his Partido Laborista to Partido Peronista. There was a reckoning coming for all this. While the effort of building up industry pleased the army and made for national pride and power, it was at the expense of neglected agriculture. Buying up foreign-owned transportation was a grand gesture, but the equipment was weary and obsolete and the price exhausted the federal reserve. Growing criticism was dealt with emphatically. Uncooperative members of the Supreme Court were impeached, universities were "renovated," with dissenters being retired, and the radio was prosecuted for *"desacato"* (disrespect), and finally put under government control. Independent labor leaders who failed to support Perón were voted down, while the army got better barracks and higher pay, with special import licenses going to favored officers.

Meanwhile, in 1947, Eva Perón obtained equal rights for women and set up charitable foundations with protection money extorted from big business, calling her efforts not charity, but an acknowledgment of the right of the poor to social justice. All this was undertaken under a new slogan, *"Justicialism,"* meaning social justice at home. It was a fine vague phrase, grandiose, modern, and patriotic. Perón had arrived.

Like Hitler, he had a flare for politics with its immediate rewards, yet none for economics, where consequences are slower to appear. Unfortunately for Perón, the foreign food market was declining. Machinery was wearing down without being replaced. He might have proceeded further with socialistic reforms. He might have expropriated the big estates. Instead, he countered growing resistance with totalitarian repression. A firm ally was lost when the church refused, upon his wife's death, to yield to his unreasonable demands that she be canonized as "Saint Eva of America." In retaliation,

Perón moved to deprive it of its tax-exempt status. When the Pope in Rome excommunicated Perón, his thugs burned down a church in Buenos Aires. This was going too far for a clique of army officers, who rose against him. Their first coup d'etat failed, but in September, 1955, another took place. Strictly military, it began in the interior and quickly spread. Rather than face a major clash, Perón left the country. Perhaps without Eva he had lost purpose. Perhaps he was mindful of what the Spanish Civil War had done to loyal labor. In any case, Perón was gone, leaving behind him economic stagnation. Agriculture was still in the hands of the traditional aristocracy, but at least the workers had higher wages, social security, and a sense of dignity and unity.

Perón has never returned to Argentina, but his ghost still haunts the land. Initially, a provisional military government took over. Generals succeeded one another in mismanaging the country until 1958, when a civilian, Arturo Frondizi, became president. Frondizi immediately wooed the Peronistas with higher wages. He continued Perón's social reforms, tried without much success to stabilize the economy, but neglected agriculture, particularly the raising of beef, which had been Argentina's biggest export. Civilian administrations followed, deriving their strength from the army: five thousand career officers, fifteen thousand career NCOs; the rest of the population do their bidding. Again in 1970 the army deposed President Organía and replaced him with Brigadier General Roberto Levingston as president by appointment, which only gave renewed support to the old joke, ''The only generals not to get their cut were General Motors and General Electric.''

Still, Argentina is basically a rich land. There is no real poverty, though public services are run down and the once proud city of Buenos Aires is shabby. The workers still revere Perón. Ignoring his Fascist oppressions and his economic failings, from which the land still suffers, they are conscious only of what he did expressly for them, those few socialistic innovations that raised them from the gutter.

Jamaica Distinct from the general Latin American development are the British, French, and Dutch islands of the Caribbean. They, too, had their Indian past, but the Indians are mostly dead and gone. Blacks from Africa have taken their place, and most of the islands that were among the British possessions have been granted their independence. Largest and most interesting from the point of view of socialism is Jamaica, which became a British possession in 1655 and had a British governor appointed in 1661. The end of slavery produced a rising black middle class, unemployment, low wages, unrest, and finally, in 1865, the beating of drums and the blowing of conch-shell horns to signal a revolt. Whites were murdered and blacks were hanged in savage reprisal. Subsequent to this Morant Bay Rebellion, reforms were undertaken and a semirepresentative government established. Among the developing parties was a labor group.

To oppose the planter-merchant oligarchy, the People's National party was founded in 1938 by Norman Washington Manley. Born in Jamaica, Manley had gone as a Rhodes scholar to Oxford and was called to the bar at Gray's Inn. He was well qualified to lead the party of progress and reform, and he saw Jamaica move from crown colony to dominion to parliamentary state within the commonwealth. During these years, his PNP declared for democratic socialism. Though suffering a setback at the exposure of a Communist cell within the party, democratic socialism gradually gobbled up a majority of the seats in Jamaica's House of Representatives. By 1959, it had a solid two-thirds majority. As prime minister, Manley launched large-scale agricultural development programs along Socialist lines. The PNP was overtaken in the mid-sixties by the National Labor party, which represents no bitter opponent and has done nothing to roll back Manley's reforms.

Mexico In background, Mexico shares much with the countries of South America: the Indian heritage, the Catholic-Spanish conquest, the nineteenth-century war of liberation, the succession of disappointing strong men that followed. Unlike the other Latin American countries, however, Mexico has already endured a major social revolution. In fact, among those twentieth-century class revolutions aimed at basic social change, Mexico's was the earliest. It was a gradual process of over one hundred years of sporadic upheaval that culminated in 1917.

The result was a one-party democracy with socialism showing better results in fact than in form. Since the revolution, Mexico has had a series of presidents handpicked by their powerful predecessors and backed by a strong party that made elective competition unrealistic. Still, criticism of the government has not been suppressed, and, despite the commonplace bribery of officials, there remains a genuine dedication to the humanitarian ends of the revolution. Initially, when the fighting died down, there were several political parties. Most faded away, leaving only the army with continuity as a political organization. It provided the early basis for establishing reform under Alvaro Obregón, the revolution's great national hero. His companion, Plutarco Elías Calles, replaced Obregón in 1924 and began gradually to shape the Partido Nacional Revolucionario. Though rival parties have been tolerated, they are no threat to its dominion.

During the revolutionary years, a powerful Socialist party had flourished in the Yucatán, where the peasants had been grossly exploited. In 1915, a liberal, General Salvador Alvarado, had gained control there with the peasants' support. Estates were confiscated and divided up among the peasantry. Subsequently, with the return of peace, socialism was reorganized along more orthodox lines and continued to lose strength. The fortunes of the party have increasingly depended on the Left or Right inclinations of the presidents. In 1934, Lázaro Cárdenas, an ex-general, was elected, and he reactivated a program of expropriation and redistribution of land. Cárdenas lived with the people and they were always his principal concern. He took over foreign-owned oil properties and gave Russian Communist Leon Trotsky political asylum. In 1937, the state nationalized the railroad system.

Today on the one hand the government of Mexico fosters a strong industrial capitalism while on the other it initiates a benevolent socialistic program. A vast and revolutionary social security system has been established, with free medical, surgical, and hospital care, support for the aged and death benefits to widows, infant care, and public housing. Appropriately, the symbol of this many-faceted system is the Mexican eagle, no longer tormenting a writhing snake, but with brooding and protective wings spread over a mother and child.

Conclusion:
Socialism's Problems
and Prospects

Socialism, even where most conscientiously applied, has by no means approximated all its ideal goals. What has been achieved has been at the price of onerous taxation and erosion of individual initiative. Even on paper, where socialism's theorists need not be limited by the realities of life, problems are admitted. Before World War I, the world seemed a simpler place, and socialism as well as those economic and social doctrines with which it competed had simple, confident answers. That simplicity is gone, taking with it the possibility of pat answers. The concern now is more with asking the right questions and choosing the most important priorities.

Some of socialism's major difficulties in practice have been with lack of incentive and mediocrity of effort on the part of managers and workers. With nationalization, the involved owner gives way to the impersonal manager. Self-interested competition is replaced by the cooperative, sheltered, cautious paper-shuffler within a state monopoly. At least in the initial phases of state ownership, the more able men are naturally attracted away into the higher-paying private sector. The question remains: will talented men work as well on salaries fixed by the government as they will when they have a sense of ownership in the company and when their income is more directly related to its success or failure? Will they jeopardize their safe positions by taking risks in the company's interest?

This dispute has been central to the status of the steel industry in Britain, where Labour placed the industry under government supervision and turned the various boards of directors into what amounted to publicly employed bureaus. The Conservatives, citing the brain drain to the United States, soon turned steel back into private hands. This issue is successfully sidestepped in Sweden, where the practice has been to tighten government supervision while leaving major industries in private ownership.

Recently, there has been a similar tendency in the United States, with the first peacetime wage and price controls, a program that is apt to see selective application continue indefinitely. Even without such government intrusion, the old days of the adventurous entrepreneur are waning fast. Big corporations today are reducing industrial innovations to routine. The Edisons are giving way to trained specialists and even to computers. The old will to die at the factory steps for the right to do as one pleases has all but gone, and the newly employed directors are not that far removed in terms of motivation from the state-controlled managers.

This incentive gap could under pure socialism exist also at lower levels. The worker, with an income fixed for life and the security of himself and his family guaranteed regardless, is apt to lean on his shovel. Aware of this problem, the more practical Socialists have recognized a need for inequality in income to spur effort. Other suggested appeals beyond the profit motive are the fear of a declining living standard and the prestige and power of the position an outstanding effort could attain. How adequately these incentives work in practice has not yet been proven.

Conclusion: Socialism's Problems and Prospects   **99**

Between management and labor, big problems remain even in a Socialist system. Under socialism, a strike would be illegal. In the United States, unions, having the power to strike, have won high wage scales with many fringe benefits, and there is genuine fear on their part that state ownership would infringe upon their rights. The solution, of course, lies in some absolute right to collective bargaining.

What about the idle and sometimes not-so-idle rich in a planned-economy system? In Soviet Russia, the answer was simple. Shoot them. Such a solution is available only under totalitarianism. Under democratic socialism, the matter becomes more complex. The rich cannot be passed off simply as overfed beasts of prey who are where they are through ruthlessness and luck and have only one function, to hold down the deserving workers. Wealth under capitalism is generally a result of effort, and such people, whatever the state's political and economic theory, are a national asset. Their wealth can't simply be expropriated. But even in the United States, heavy income, estate, and gift taxation tend to keep it in check. Yet questions remain. How heavy can such taxation become without acting as a restraint on enterprise? Then there are the people outside the manager-worker framework. There are the professional men, lawyers and doctors. Perhaps Britain's National Health Service is an answer for the United States medical profession, but what of artists and writers? If they are to have a set wage, how are the gifted to be separated from the drones? Professional athletes? Will team spirit compensate for reduced earnings?

A major debate among economists has to do with pricing where a free market does not exist. Socialism would substitute a controlled price for that price determined by supply and demand in a free capitalist market. There are major questions of where adjustments would be made with the likelihood that either freedom of consumer's choice or that of occupation would be interfered with. Socialist economists insist that prices would be adjusted according to surplus or deficit by a series of trials and errors as in the capitalist system. Final decisions would be left to a central pricing board with the task not of dictating prices, but of responding to consumers' demands.

Socialism has never thought of itself as simply a national or economic structure. It has always aspired to international influence of a pacifistic nature. In practice, democratic socialism has found itself caught between a devotion to democracy and a general historical sympathy with the social and economic order that communism seeks but that has in fact been defiled by totalitarian tactics. Like communism, democratic socialism has entirely underrated the part nationalism plays in influencing world conditions, and this blind spot has tended to paralyze socialism on the international level. Traditionally, wars have been blamed on capitalism, and only recently have Democratic Socialists recognized the militant role of fascism and communism and the sad truth that the causes of war are far more complex and widespread than the selfish ambitions of munitions manufacturers.

Socialists have had approximately a century to solve the world's problems. They have less certain answers now than they had a hundred years ago, for the world is very different from that of Robert Owen, Charles Fourier, and John Stuart Mill. As of 1914, the world was controlled by a few powerful nations and empires. Now one hundred and thirty-odd sovereign nations exist, equal with each other in theory, if not always in fact. Since World War II, only Russia has expanded her empire, under the pretext of Communist concern for freeing her satellites from capitalist bondage. Where new freedom has come, particularly in Africa and Asia, it has meant primarily bread and perhaps a crumb of cake, not the Westernized prerogative to know, to utter, and to argue freely, according to conscience. Democracy in this philosophical sense is an unknown and unsavored virtue and at best a secondary concern. However vague and blundering socialism may be, the planned and in part nationalized economy seems to offer the best hope of rapid advancement for these underdeveloped countries. In the industrialized nations, there has been a slow drift toward socialistic techniques if not toward socialism itself simply because the enormous complexity of modern business and society requires government guidance in order to function.

In the United States, socialism has always been regarded as more of a threat than a promise, and indications of its encroachment have been recognized with antagonism. This swing toward socialism is not the result of some secret conspiracy or dedicated cadre of ideology pushers. It represents the unavoidable evolution of twentieth-century society. To resent this change is to give in to nostalgia for the good old days, which may, indeed, have been better, but, like every man's youth, are gone forever. The United States has absorbed its frontier. The local candlestick- and carriage-makers have become General Electric and the Ford Motor Company. Vanished is the land of small farmers and shopkeepers. The advance of science and industry has made for big business. As a reaction, and in order to survive, has come big labor, big shopkeeping, and big government. One demands the other, and it is unavoidable that modern government must arbitrate where possible between the competing interests of business, labor, and the public.

In industrialized Europe as well as in emergent nations, the tendency has been toward government economic planning. Immediately one thinks of the much-propagandized five-year plans of the Soviet Union, with their disregard of individualism, and such thoughts give planning a bad name. However, government planning need not be compulsory or aimed solely at developing heavy industry or basic agriculture. It does not even require a Socialist government to operate effectively. France, for instance, has initiated a kind of noncollectivist planning for general economic growth, and its results are achieved through consultation between unions, business, and government agencies. Without any compulsory elements, this system has demonstrated that planning, even if merely a system of proposing goals and exchanging information, can stimulate the economy.

Along with social security, the minimum wage, and other socialistic devices, some form of economic planning and coordination, however disguised or soft-pedaled, does take place in the United States and will increasingly do so. Inflation must be controlled, along with the absurd cost of medical care. The consumer must be protected against irresponsible and sometimes dangerous advertising. Most serious of all, there is the endangering of the natural environment by industrial waste and growing population. No matter how many beer cans boy scouts may pick up on Earth Day, this deteriorating situation must presently fall under stern governmental, perhaps international, controls. This trend need not be feared as socialism simply because the Socialists first conceived the idea. It should be seen as a valuable tool necessary in dealing with any complex modern society, for no matter how much we lament their passing, times permitting unrestricted rugged individualism are gone.

Briefly, then, what are the prospects of this democratic socialism, which walks a tightrope between communism on one side and capitalism on the other? Both extremes are enemies of socialism. Capitalism is the old foe that gave socialism birth. With the years these two have learned a certain mutual tolerance, even grudging respect. Communism remains a far more bitter rival. As Lenin once said, ''Social Democrats are to Communists what rope is to a condemned man.'' The sentiment is mutual. At a recent meeting of International Socialism in Helsinki, Chile's new Marxist president, Salvador Allende Gossens, was denied a seat when West Germany's Socialist Chancellor Willy Brandt made Allende's absence a condition of his own attendance.

Conclusion: Socialism's Problems and Prospects   **103**

Bertrand Russell, looking back on the havoc of the First World War once said, ''The war and its sequel have proved the destructiveness of capitalism; let us see to it that the next epoch does not prove the still greater destructiveness of communism, but rather the power of socialism to heal the wounds which the old evil system has inflicted upon the human spirit.'' He blamed capitalism too completely for the world's troubles while having no reason as yet to fear another "ism" that was already incubating in Italy and Germany. The destructiveness of communism seems hopefully now in check, but Russell's hope for world socialism still awaits a final verdict. Certainly it is an influential doctrine offering social and economic structures needed in developing as well as in highly industrialized countries, while at the same time offering a compromise between capitalism and communism. It may, indeed, represent the wave of the future, but, in every ocean, each wave is followed by another, and waves merge and dissipate. There are today other forces for revolutionary change still in their infancy: science, cybernetics, nuclear power, population explosion, all the controlled or controllable forces of nature that are changing the world.

Definitions

Chartists   Members of a nineteenth-century British movement that demanded a national charter to guarantee the workingman political and economic rights. *See also* People's Charter.

Diggers   Seventeenth-century English socialists who wished to return to the simple life of the days following creation and demonstrated this desire by digging up parks and commons.

Fabian Society   An English intellectual group, founded in 1884, devoted to the advocacy of gradual pragmatic socialism. Members included G. B. Shaw and H. G. Wells.

Fourierism   A utopian plan for communal living devised by Frenchman Charles Fourier in the early nineteenth century and tried out unsuccessfully in the United States at Brook Farm, Massachusetts, among other places. Under this system society was organized into groups called phalansteries, each large enough to provide for all the material and social needs of the members.

Histadrut   Israel's general labor federation.

Kibbutzim   Communal settlements organized in Israel for purposes of production and defense.

Levellers Seventeenth-century English group that wanted to put an end to the monarchy and return to a communal form of living.

Moshavim Settlements in Israel featuring cooperation between small landholders in renting heavy equipment and marketing produce.

Nationalization The objective of Communists and some Socialists to move the means of production and distribution from private to public ownership.

Negritude A sense of blackness developed among black Africans, creating a feeling of spiritual unity.

New Atlantis A utopian community described by Francis Bacon in the book *New Atlantis*.

New Lanark A Scottish mill town, reformed by Robert Owen with his socialistic innovations during the early nineteenth century.

Paris Commune An insurgent group of French workers, wanting to set up a federation of communes, who seized Paris in 1871, at the end of the Franco-Prussian War. They held the city for three months until ruthlessly suppressed by the French Army.

People's Charter Drawn up in 1838 by the British Working Men's Association to guarantee reforms along socialist lines. It collected a large following—the Chartists—and though a source of agitation for several years was never enacted.

Phalanstery A Fourierist community. *See also* Fourierism.

Revisionism A term originally applied by Communists to Eduard Bernstein's modifications of Marxism along Fabian lines.

Rochdale weavers A group of English weavers who in the mid-nineteenth century initiated a cooperative movement that has spread enormously while encouraging numerous similar projects.

Shirtless Ones Gangs of Argentinian workers who supported Juan Perón.

Socialism of the Chair Socialist ideas advanced in the late nineteenth century by a group of German university professors.

"Sweater" One who obtained labor for the clothing merchants in mid-nineteenth-century Britain. He furnished the workers with housing at such a cost as to keep them hopelessly in debt.

Syndicalism A revolutionary labor movement of the late nineteenth century that advocated the general workers' strike that would lead to control of the government.

Utopia Any intellectually conceived ideal community organized for the general welfare. The term derives from such a community pictured in Thomas More's book *Utopia*.

Welfare state The national conception of government responsibility to maintain public services and a minimum living standard for all citizens.

Young Turk A phrase used to identify a member of a twentieth-century revolutionary group in Turkey, and since used of a radical insurgent of any political party.

Biographies

Adler, Viktor (1852–1918): Founder of the Austrian Social Democratic party. His son Friedrich assassinated Count Karl von Stürgkh, the premier of Austria.

Attlee, Clement R. (1883–1967): British Labour party leader. Prime minister following the Second World War who initiated Socialist programs.

Babeuf, François Émile (1760–1797): Socialist writer and political activist at the time of the French Revolution.

Bacon, Francis (1561–1626): English philosopher and author. In 1622 he wrote *New Atlantis,* setting out a utopian paradise along socialist lines.

Ball, John (died 1381): An English priest who taught the doctrines of Wycliffe, and for his part in the Wat Tyler rebellion was executed.

Bebel, August (1840–1913): German author who took part in founding the German Democratic party and later became its leader.

Bernstein, Eduard (1850–1932): German Social Democratic politician and writer who led the modification of Marxian socialism from a policy of revolution to one of evolution.

Betancourt, Rómulo (1908–   ): Socialistic leader in Venezuela who resisted dictatorship there. Elected president in 1958, he did much to stabilize democratic socialism in that country.

Bismarck, Prince Otto Eduard Leopold von (1815–1898): Known as the Iron Chancellor of Germany, he achieved many economic and social reforms in that country. Among these were a form of workmen's compulsory insurance and the federal ownership of key industries. He has been called the father of the modern welfare state.

Blanc, Louis (1811–1882): During the French Revolution of 1848 Blanc was a member of the provisional government. Though his policy of guaranteed employment for the workers was not adopted he is still regarded as the father of state socialism.

Blum, Léon (1872–1950): French politician. Leader of Socialist party and then of the Popular Front. Became premier in 1936 and during World War II was a prisoner of the Nazis.

Bolívar, Simón (1783–1830): Known as the George Washington of South America, he was a major factor in that continent's liberation from Spain. Later his efforts at governing Venezuela democratically failed and he became a dictator before being driven into exile.

Brandt, Willy (1913–   ): German Socialist who fled the country during the Nazi regime to escape arrest. In 1957 he became the mayor of West Berlin. Throughout the 1960s he was the leader of the Social Democratic party and was elected chancellor in 1969.

Bryan, William Jennings (1860–1925): Known as "the Commoner." A reformer, he ran for President repeatedly as a Democrat and was instrumental in getting the nomination for Woodrow Wilson in 1912. Later Bryan became secretary of state but could not support the drift toward World War I involvement and resigned the post.

Cárdenas, Lázaro (1895–   ): Mexican soldier and radical leader; he became president of Mexico in 1934 when he launched a six-year plan for redistribution of land.

Cole, George Douglas Howard (1889–1959): English economist and novelist, author of many books on socialism and chairman of the Fabian Society after World War II.

Debs, Eugene Victor (1855–1926): Leader in the Pullman strike,

1894. Three years later organized the Social Democratic party of America and ran as a Socialist for President of the United States in 1900, 1904, 1908, 1912, 1920.

Dollfuss, Engelbert (1892–1934): Austrian statesman who tried to preserve Austrian independence by declaring a dictatorship. Austrian Nazis subsequently shot him.

Emerson, Ralph Waldo (1803–1882): American poet and essayist. He participated in the Brook Farm experiment in communal living.

Fourier, François Marie Charles (1772–1837): Social theorist and utopian reformer who structured a cooperative society in which the members all lived in a single building. In practice these phalansteries were not a success.

Franco, Francisco (1892–   ): Spanish soldier and dictator. He led the Fascist cause to victory in the 1936 rebellion and became the country's dictator thereafter.

Gandhi, Mohandas Karamchand (1869–1948): Hindu nationalist leader who campaigned against British colonialism in India with a program of civil disobedience. Called Mahatma.

Kingsley, Charles (1819–1875): English clergyman and novelist. Sympathized with the Chartists and worked for Christian socialism.

Lassalle, Ferdinand (1812–1864): German Socialist. Championed the working classes, proposed setting up cooperative associations, and is regarded as the founder of the German Social Democratic party.

Leo XIII (1810–1903): Gioacchino Pecci. Pope from 1878 until 1903, during which time was published his encyclical *Rerum novarum* (1891) discussing modern socialism.

Lloyd George, David (1863–1945): British statesman. Prime minister from 1916–1922, directed the war effort and instituted social reforms.

Mboya, Tom (1930–1969): Leading economic and social theorist in Kenya. In 1963 he became minister of economic planning and development. A likely candidate to succeed President Kenyatta, he was assassinated in 1969.

Mill, John Stuart (1806–1873): English philosopher and economist whose convictions gradually evolved toward socialism.

More, Thomas (1478–1535): English statesman and social philosopher, canonized a Catholic saint. The author of *Utopia,* among other works. When he refused to accept Henry VIII's assumption of jurisdiction over the church of England, in place of the Pope, he was charged with treason and decapitated.

Mussolini, Benito (1883–1945): Socialist turned Fascist, he became dictator of Italy. On April 28, 1945, he was executed by Italian partisans.

Nasser, Gamal Abdel (1918–1970): Soldier and a member of the officers' clique that deposed King Farouk I. Later he became president of Egypt, as the United Arab Republic (then including Syria), and instituted reforms under a program that he described as Arab socialism.

Nehru, Jawaharlal (1889–1964): Indian nationalist leader and follower of Gandhi, who succeeded Gandhi as leader of the National Congress party. Later he became prime minister.

Obregón, Alvaro (1880–1928): Mexican politician and soldier. Hero of the revolution, he became president of Mexico in 1920. Elected again in 1928, he was promptly assassinated.

Owen, Robert (1771–1858): Industrialist and labor reformer. He founded a number of cooperative settlements both in England and the United States. New Harmony, Indiana, is the best remembered of these earnest "Owenite" failures.

Perón, Juan Domingo (1895–   ): Argentine politician, minister of war, and secretary of labor. As president of Argentina he instituted popular reforms; overthrown by the army and exiled to Spain.

Pius XI (1857–1939): Achille Ratti. Pope from 1922 until 1939. He favored socialism over modern monopoly capitalism, expressing his thinking in the encyclical *Quadragesimo anno* (1931).

Proudhon, Pierre Joseph (1809–1865): French radical and author, regarded today by many as the founder of anarchism.

Ripley, George (1802–1880): American social reformer who founded Brook Farm, an experiment in communal living.

Saint-Simon, Claude Henri (1760–1825): French social scientist and philosopher. He is considered the founder of French socialism.

Shaw, George Bernard (1856–1950): British playwright, novelist, and social critic, leading socialist, member of the Fabian Society.

Thomas, Norman Mattoon (1884–1968): American Socialist who ran repeatedly for the presidency. He wrote a number of books on the subject of socialism.

Wells, Herbert George (1866–1946): English novelist, writer on sociology, and member of the Fabian Society.

Wycliffe, John (1320?–1384): Wycliffe is remembered for his attempts to deprive the church of its temporal powers. His aggitations provoked the peasants into an uprising that was harshly suppressed.

Bibliography of Sources

Black, Clinton. *The Story of Jamaica*. London: Collins, 1965.

Braatoy, Bjarne. *The New Sweden: A Vindication of Democracy*. New York: Thomas Nelson, 1939.

Callahan, Daniel. *The New Church—Essays in Catholic Reform*. New York: Scribner, 1965.

Chase, Stuart. *The Most Probable World*. New York: Harper & Row, 1968.

Cole, G. D. H. *The Life of Robert Owen*. New York: Macmillan, 1930.

———. *The Fabian Society, Past and Present*. London: The Fabian Society, 1942.

———. *World Socialism Restated*. London, Turnstile Press, 1956.

Eaton, John. *Socialism in the Nuclear Age*. London: Lawrence & Wishart, 1961.

Edwards, Harvey. *Scandinavia: The Challenge of Welfare*. New York: Thomas Nelson, 1968.

Engels, Friedrich. *Socialism: Utopian and Scientific*. New York: International Publishers, 1933.

Fremantle, Anne. *This Little Band of Prophets: The British Fabians*. New York: New American Library, 1959.

Fromm, Erich, Ed. *Socialist Humanism: An International Symposium.* New York: Doubleday, 1965.

Gay, Peter. *The Dilemma of Democratic Socialism.* New York: Columbia University Press, 1952.

Gregg, Pauline. *The Welfare State.* Boston: University of Massachusetts Press, 1969.

Grimley, O. B. *The New Norway.* Oslo: Griff-Forlaget, 1937.

Hackett, Francis. *I Chose Denmark.* New York: Doubleday, 1941.

Halpern, Manfred. *The Politics of Social Change in the Middle East and North Africa.* Princeton, N.J.: Princeton University Press, 1963.

Hart, Madge. *Utopias—Old and New.* London: T. Nelson & Sons, 1932.

Laidler, Harry. *History of Socialism.* New York: Thomas Y. Crowell, 1968.

Lloyd, P. C. *Africa in Social Change.* New York: Praeger, 1967.

Loucks, William N. and Whitney, William G. *Comparative Economic Systems.* New York: Harper & Row, 1965.

Mumford, Lewis. *The Story of Utopias.* New York: Boni & Liveright, 1922.

Niebuhr, Reinhold. *Man's Nature and His Communities.* New York: Scribner, 1965.

Pike, Frederick B. *The Modern History of Peru.* New York: Praeger, 1967.

Putnam, John. *The Modern Case for Socialism.* Boston: Meador Publishing Co., 1943.

Schumpeter, Joseph, *Capitalism, Socialism and Democracy.* New York: Harper & Brothers, 1942.

Senghor, Léopold S. *On African Socialism.* New York: Praeger, 1964.

Simpson, Colin. *The Viking Circle.* New York: Fielding Publications Inc., 1968.

Sturmthal, Adolf. *The Tragedy of European Labor.* New York: Columbia University Press, 1943.

Thomas, Norman. *Socialism Re-examined.* New York: W. W. Norton & Co., 1963.

Tilman, Robert O. *Man, State, and Society in Contemporary Southeast Asia.* New York: Praeger, 1969.

Vatikiotis, P. J., Ed. *Egypt Since the Revolution.* New York: Praeger, 1968.

Voorhis, Jerry. *American Cooperatives.* New York: Harper & Row, 1961.

Westmeyer, Russel E. *Modern Economic and Social Systems.* New York: Farrar & Rinehart, 1940.

Whitaker, Arthur P. *Argentina.* Englewood Cliffs, N.J.: Prentice-Hall, 1964.

Index

INDEX

122

Histadrut, 54
Hitler, Adolf, 38
Holland
    Catholic People's party,
      44
    Social Democratic Union,
      43-44
Holyoake, Keith, 72
Hornsrud, Christian, 45
Hungarian Revolution (1956),
    34

Incentive gap, 98-99
Independent Labour party
    (Great Britain), 25
Independent Socialist party
    (Argentina), 91
India
    agriculture, 68-70
    Congress party, 66-67
    Congress Socialist
      party, 66
    economic planning, 67-
      69
    five-year plans, 68-70
    foreign aid, 70
    Great Britain and, 65-66
    independence, 65-66
    industry, 68, 70
    Pakistan and, 71
    population, 67-68
    religious rivalry, 66
Industrial Revolution, 10, 19,
    29

Industry
    coal, 13-14
    India, 68, 70
    Ireland, 27
    nationalization, 5, 7, 13-
      15, 99
    steel, 14-15
    Sweden, 48-49
    United States, 82
Inflation, 8
Ireland, 27-28
Iron and Steel Act (1949),
    14-15
Iron and Steel Corporation
    of Great Britain, 15
Israel
    Arabs and, 52
    cooperative system, 21
    Histadrut, 54
    kibbutzim, 51-53
    Labor party, 54
    Mapai, 53
    moshavim, 53
    statehood, 53
Italy
    Communist party, 42
    fascism, 41-42
    Matteotti Affair, 41
    Socialist party, 41-42

Jainism, 64
Jamaica, 95-96
Japan, 75-76
Jaurès, Jean, 6, 33

Shirtless Ones, 92
Sikhism, 64
Sinclair, Upton, 79
Sindri Fertilizer Corporation, 70
Slavery, 58, 78
Social Credit party (New Zealand), 72
Social Democratic party
    Austria, 39-41
    Denmark, 46-47
    Finland, 47-48
    Germany, 35-39
    Japan, 76
    Sweden, 45
    U. S., 79-80
Social Democratic Union (Holland), 43-44
Social Democratic Working-men's Party (Germany), 36
Social Labor party (Spain), 42
Social Masses party (Japan), 75
Socialism of the Chair, 37
Socialist Information and Liaison Office, 7
Socialist Labor party
    Argentina, 91
    Canada, 77-78
    Chile, 86
    U. S., 79
Socialist League (Japan), 75
Socialist party
    Burma, 71-72

France, 33-35
    Italy, 41-42
Socialist Program party (Burma), 72
"Socialized Medicine", 15-16
Sorel, Georges, 33
Spaak, Paul-Henri, 44
Spain, 27, 84
    fascism, 42-43
    Social Labor party, 42
Spanish Civil War, 92
Spence, Thomas, 19
Steel industry, 14-15
Storting (Norway), 45
Stürgkh, Count, 40
Suez Canal, 56
Sweater, 23
Sweden, 99
    cooperative system, 21, 49
    industry, 48-49
    Social Democratic party, 45
    welfare programs, 44, 48
Switzerland, Grütli Union, 43
Syndicalism, 5, 32-33
Syria, 55

Temple, William, 11
"Thirty Comrades", 71
Thomas, Norman, 79-80
Town and Country Planning Act (1932), 12

About the Author

James D. Forman is a well-known author of books for young people, among them *Shield of Achilles, Ring the Judas Bell,* and *My Enemy, My Brother.* The last two titles were honored in the *Book World* Spring Book Festival in the year of their publication.

Mr. Forman is a graduate of Princeton University and Columbia University Law School. He has traveled widely in Europe, especially in Greece, a country that has served as background for a number of his books. Mr. Forman lives on Long Island.